EXPLORING BIBLE LANGUAGE

Alan and Margaret Fowler

Ortho Books
High View, Litchard Rise
BRIDGEND CF31 1QJ, UK.

Copyright 1996 Alan and Margaret Fowler

ISBN 0 9529114 1 8

Printed by:
Printland Publishers, G.P.O. Box 159, Hyderabad, 500 001, India who are also the agents for India and Australasia.

Agents for the Americas:
1. Mr. Forrest Brinkerhoff, 565 South Traffic Way, Arroyo Grande, California, 93420, U.S.A. Ph. (805) 481 - 228
2. Mrs. I Schneider, 1015 Symington Ave., Baltimore, Maryland, 21228, U.S.A. Ph. (410) 747 - 5760

Cover photo: Qumran Caves where the Dead Sea Scrolls were found.

Acknowledgments

Frontispiece Poem from Llanrhaeadr - ym - Mochnant in *Welsh Airs*, 1987. Kind permission of the author and Poetry Wales Press.

Quotations from the NKJV by kind permission of Thomas Nelson Inc. Copyright © 1982.

Quotations from the NRSV by kind permission of the National Council of the Churches of Christ in the USA. Copyright © 1989.

We are grateful to Vera Watkins for producing the original typescript and to Elvin Nix for producing the final copy for the printer.

We are also grateful to our readers, Joseph Fowler, Sheila Harris and Bert Twelves for many valuable criticisms and corrections.

Abbreviations

v.	verse
Ch.	chapter
Heb.	Hebrew
Gk.	Greek
N.T.	New Testament
O.T.	Old Testament
KJV	King James Version (1611)
RV	Revised Version (1884)
RSV	Revised Standard Version (1952)
NEB	New English Bible (1970)
GNB	Good News Bible (1976)
NIV	New International Version (1978)
NKJV	New King James Version (1982)
NJB	New Jerusalem Bible (1985)
REB	Revised English Bible (1989)
NRSV	New Revised Standard Version (1989)

CONTENTS

Foreward viii

Chapter   **Page**

1   The Problem and its Solution 1

PART 1   **WORDS** 9

2   Extracting the Meaning 11
        'For ever' 12
3   "In the image of God He created him" 16
4   "The whole creation groans" 18
5   "In sorrow thou shalt bring forth children" 21
6   "The word was made flesh" 24
7   "By whom he made the worlds" 28
8   'Son of God' 32
9   "In my Father's house are many mansions" 38
10   Adultery and fornication 41

PART 2   **FIGURES OF SPEECH** 47

11   IDIOM 49
12   Knowledge of Good and Evil 51
13   Infinitive Absolute 54
                The Tree of Life 54
                Punishments of Genesis 3 57
14   Idioms for the Superlative 64
15   Comparative Negative 66
                'Not to baptize' 66
                'Hate father and mother' 67
                "Does God care for oxen?" 67
                'Not against flesh and blood' 69
                'Not with braided hair ...' 70
16   Emphatic "today" 71
                The Penitent Thief 71
                'Spirits in Prison' 82
                Homoeoteluton error 84

17	METAPHOR	86
	In John's Gospel	87
	'The Sleep of Death'	88
18	Flesh	89
19	Hell	94
20	Heaven(s) and Earth	100
21	Divine anthropomorphism and condescension	106
22	METONYMY	110
23	IRONY	113
24	"Here are two swords"	116
25	The unjust steward & the rich man & Lazarus	121
26	CONCESSION	126
27	HYPERBOLE	128
28	UNIVERSALIST LANGUAGE and the Flood	131
29	PERSONIFICATION: Satan in the Old Testament	136
30	Satan and devil in the New Testament	142
	The serpent in Eden	149
31	ELLIPSIS	153
32	PROLEPSIS	160

PART 3 STYLE AND STRUCTURE OF LANGUAGE ... 163

33	PROSE AND POETRY	165
34	Hyperbole	169
	Joshua's long day	171
35	DRAMA	175
	Job	176
	Song of Solomon	178
	Temptation of Jesus Christ	179
	Song of Deborah	182
36	Days of Creation	184

PART 4 VERB FORMS ... 193

37	Imprecatory Psalms	195
38	The Fatal Spear Thrust	199
39	Conclusion	207

Index of Scripture Quotations ... 211

There is no portrait of him,
But in the gallery of
The imagination; a brow
With the hair's feathers
Spilled on it; a cheek
Too hollow; rows of teeth
Broken on the unmanageable bone
Of language.

R S Thomas on William Morgan,
the first translator of the Welsh Bible

FOREWARD

It would be a great pity if any reader formed the impression that the Bible demands a high degree of scholarship to understand the gospel of personal salvation. This is not a book on theology; its aim is to show that the Bible is its own interpreter. In this way it will show that many of the concepts of popular theology are not supported by the Bible. These erroneous interpretations arise because people read into the Bible their own preconceptions and prejudices. They fail to treat the Bible as a whole and do not follow the golden rule which is to compare one part of the Bible with another.

Some of our conclusions may surprise or even offend. We claim no infallibility so would welcome comment and criticism from our readers.

CHAPTER 1

THE PROBLEM AND ITS SOLUTION

There are three important endowments which distinguish man from the animals:

1. Man can think outside of himself; he is self-conscious, seeing himself as part of a larger creation. This means he is also God-conscious, feeling himself under the influence of unseen forces.

2. Man can think outside the present time. He is aware of the past and can anticipate the future. As a result he can consciously learn lessons from the past and deliberately plan for the future. The contrast between man and the animals in relation to time is beautifully expressed by Robert Burns in his poem, *"To a Mouse"*:

> Still thou art blessed, compared wi' me!
> The present only toucheth thee:
> But, och! I backward cast my e'e
> On prospects drear!
> And forward, though I canna see,
> I guess and fear.

3. Man can express his thoughts in language and this provides a vehicle for thought. "Thought, in the sense of understanding, is helpless without words — it can't get moving."[1] Because language is the vehicle of thought it is clearly the most important of the qualities that distinguish man from beasts.

---

1. Douglas Spanner, *Biblical Creation and the Theory of Evolution*, p.63.

Although apes can be taught to recognize and respond to more than 20 words there is no evidence that they can use words to construct sentences. Many attempts have been made to get chimpanzees to talk but reported instances of language are found to be no more than elaborate tricks for obtaining rewards. Language is unique to man. "Man's vocal organs, lungs and brains are 'pre-set' to cope with the intricacies of speech in much the same way that monkeys are pre-set to climb trees and bats to squeak."[1]

Language can be recorded visually in the form of writing. Writing has the advantage over speech in that thoughts (facts, opinions, instructions, etc.) can be stored for future use either by the writer or by other people. Through the written word man is able to accumulate huge deposits (libraries) of knowledge. This means that he is able to advance his knowledge by building on the experience of past generations. By learning from the past we make a tool to shape the future. Whenever we refuse to learn from the experience of others we confirm the truth of the proverb, "Experience is the school of fools".[2] The Bible is essentially a library of divinely inspired knowledge and wisdom recorded for the guidance of present and future generations. It is the height of folly for us to spurn this storehouse of divine wisdom.

Bible truths were expressed in contemporary language. Although guided by the Spirit of God, authors of the Bible spoke and wrote in the language of their hearers. Otherwise, how could the message be understood by their contemporaries? So our first task in the search for Bible truth is to find the most reliable copies of the original writings. We must then determine what the authors meant by what they wrote. It would be wrong to assume that even if we had an exact copy of what was written we should automatically understand what the writer intended to convey.

---

1. Jean Aitchison, *The Articulate Mammal*, Second Edition, 1983, p.76.

2. According to the *Concise Oxford Dictionary of Proverbs* (1992) this proverb appears in R. Ascham, *Schoolmaster* (1570), "Erasmus ... saide wiselie that experience is the common scholehouse of foles."

"Do you understand what you are reading?" (Acts 8:30)

The Gospel of John reveals how easily language can be misunderstood. The words of Jesus were repeatedly misinterpreted by both friend and foe. Here are some examples:

Ch. 2:19: Jesus says, "Destroy this temple and in three days I will raise it up." The Jews thought he was referring to the temple building but he was, of course, speaking of the temple of his body (v.21).

Ch. 3:5-10: Jesus tells Nicodemus, "... unless one is born again, he cannot see the Kingdom of God." Nicodemus replies, "How can a man be born when he is old?" Jesus rebukes Nicodemus for his lack of understanding: "Are you a teacher of Israel, and do not know these things?"

Ch. 4:10-14: Jesus tells the woman at the well that he could give her 'living water'. She replies, "Sir, you have nothing to draw with, and the well is deep." Jesus explains that he is talking about a quality of life (v.14).

Ch. 6:51-57: Jesus says, "I am the living bread which came down from heaven. If anyone eats of this bread, he will live for ever." The Jews retort, "How can this man give us his flesh to eat?" Jesus later explains that he was using spiritual language and that the literal flesh profits nothing (v. 63).

Ch. 8:21-30: Jesus says, "I am going away ... where I go you cannot come." The Jews thought he was talking of suicide whereas he was speaking of his eventual ascension into heaven.

Ch. 11:11-14: Jesus says concerning the dead Lazarus, "Our friend Lazarus sleeps." The disciples say, "Lord, if he sleeps he will get well." Then Jesus speaks plainly, "Lazarus is dead."

Ch. 16:16-29: Jesus says, "A little while and you will not see me; and again a little while, and you will see me ...". The disciples are baffled by this language so Jesus explains that he is referring to the Holy Spirit which he will give them after he had gone away. The disciples then exclaim with relief, "See, now you are speaking plainly, *and using no figure of speech!*"[1]

Ch. 21:22-23: Jesus continues to speak cryptically right up to the end. When Peter asks Jesus about John, Jesus replies, "If I will that he remain until I come, what is that to you? You follow me." They thought this referred to the fact that John would not die but later they would know that Jesus was probably referring to the revelation which he gave John on the Isle of Patmos.

So we see that although they heard the actual words of Jesus, both his friends and foes often misunderstood what he meant. So we should not be surprised that those who read the Bible almost 2,000 years later may have similar problems.

The Causes of Misunderstanding Today

The fact that we are reading rather than hearing the words does nothing to diminish the problem; in some ways it increases the difficulties. According to Bacon, "Reading maketh a full man, conference a ready man and writing an *exact* man." But paradoxically, although a writer will know exactly what he means, the reader can easily misunderstand him. There are four principal reasons for this:

---

1. The KJV has 'proverb' here. The Greek word is *paroimia* (literally, 'wayside saying'). It is used only in John 10:6, John 16:25 and 29 and 2 Pet. 2:22. The *paroimiai* or 'sayings' of John's Gospel must be distinguished from parables and allegories. In the New Testament a parable, from the Greek *parabolē* (lit. 'placing beside'), is a *story* with a hidden meaning whereas allegory, from the Greek *allēgoreō* (lit. 'I speak otherwise'), is *history* with a hidden meaning, as in Gal.4:24. See also end of Ch. 21.

(1) Words may have more than one meaning and their meanings can change with the passage of time.

(2) All languages use figures of speech which may easily be misunderstood.

(3) Writing may be used in different styles and structures, namely prose, poetry and drama. A recognition of the category may be needed to understand the meaning.

(4) Some tenses in the original Bible languages can be ambiguous and need care in translation.

Although we shall discuss these problems in separate sections of the book there will often be some overlap in considering a difficult passage of Scripture.

Principles of Interpretation

In seeking to understand the language of the Bible there are four possible lines of approach: 1. take every word at its face value, i.e. literally, 2. accept the interpretation of an 'authority', e.g. a theologian or Church, 3. seek prayerfully for Divine guidance, 4. adopt the principle that the Bible interprets itself. These different approaches are not mutually exclusive but only the fourth is totally reliable.

1. Taking all parts of the Bible literally cannot be right, as shown in examples from the gospel of John. Most of the book of Revelation is symbolic and much of the Old Testament is written in poetry and abounds in figurative language. Bible exposition is often marred by a failure to appreciate that its language is not always plain. The language of the Bible is often very complex and makes demands on our understanding. The Bible is true but it is not always literally true. Taking the Bible literally in all its parts shows no understanding of the subtlety of Bible language and no respect for Bible truth.

2. The suggestion that we should leave the interpretation of Scripture to the 'experts' or defer to the authority of a particular church is an easy option that appeals to many, but it is fraught with pitfalls. If we believe that the Bible is the word of God then we need to be very cautious in accepting the authority of any human institution. By so doing we are in danger of allowing fallible human judgment to usurp divine authority. Churches often interpret the Bible differently in spite of each claiming to be guided by the Holy Spirit.

3. Though we commend a personal and prayerful approach to Bible exposition, we must accept that we are fallible and recognize that many who claim Divine guidance do not always reach the same conclusions.

4. Since we cannot be sure that any human interpretation is correct we must give priority to the principle that the Bible interprets itself.

If the Bible is wholly inspired and infallible it cannot contradict itself and must be consistent in all its parts. Referring to the O.T., Peter tells us that "men moved by the Holy Spirit spoke from God" (2 Pet. 1:21). And Jesus promised his apostles that the Holy Spirit would teach them all things (John 14:26). Since the whole Bible was written under the guidance of the Holy Spirit we should expect to find harmony between all parts of Scripture. So the best way to understand a difficult word or passage will be by comparing Scripture with Scripture, which Paul described as "comparing spiritual things with spiritual" (1 Cor. 2:13).

To compare Scripture with Scripture we must first look at the context. This may be a paragraph, a chapter, or even several chapters. In many cases this will provide us with enough clues to determine the meaning. But if there remains any doubt, we must then broaden our enquiry and examine how the same words or phrases are used in other parts of the same book of the Bible or in other books by the same author. Finally our enquiry may involve investigation of teaching on the same subject in other parts of Scripture.

This principle of allowing Scripture to interpret Scripture will be our approach and in this way we hope to show that satisfactory answers may be found to many problems of Scripture interpretation. We do not expect all our readers to agree with all our conclusions. We shall be content if we can persuade the reader to accept that in a search for Bible truth we must not only seek to discover exactly what was originally written but must also humbly seek to understand the writer's intention by comparing Scripture with Scripture and allowing the Bible to interpret itself.

Obviously we cannot deal with all the problems which arise as we read through the Bible. The examples chosen will be those which illustrate the importance of understanding language in our search for fundamental Bible truths.

In spite of some theological bias in the King James Version (KJV) and the New King James Version (NKJV) we have often used them because they are more literal translations[1] than the Revised Version (RV), Revised Standard Version (RSV), New Revised Standard Version (NRSV), New English Bible (NEB), Revised English Bible (REB) and Good News Bible (GNB). However, in a book such as this, the choice of translation is not so important because the quotations are subjected to linguistic and Biblical analysis. Unless otherwise stated the NKJV is used.

---

1. There are four categories of translation: 1. *Interlinear* or word for word as in the NT *Emphatic Diaglott*, 2. *formal equivalence* using the grammar and idioms of the original as in the KJV, 3. *dynamic equivalence* using the grammar and idiom of the receptor language as in most modern English versions and 4. *paraphrase* i.e. with added explanation as in the GNB.

PART 1

WORDS

CHAPTER 2

EXTRACTING THE MEANING

Words are the currency of language but many of them cannot be stamped with a definite value. As we have emphasized, words may have more than one meaning and they tend to change their meanings with the passage of time. A glance at a dictionary will reveal that many words have deviated from their origins and some have even acquired opposite meanings, such as 'presently' which originally meant 'immediately'. For this reason dictionaries have to be constantly revised, and they are of little value in determining the meanings of words used thousands of years ago.

Moreover, the difficulty is compounded by using a translation because we then have the additional problem of understanding the meaning of the words used by the translator. The KJV translation, for example, contains more than 300 words whose meanings have substantially changed since it was first published in 1611. The KJV uses the word *let* in the sense of hinder, *prevent* for precede, *conversation* for conduct, *comprehend* for overcome, *wealth* for wellbeing, *allege* for prove, *demand* for ask, *doctrine* for teaching, etc.

By going back to the original Hebrew and Greek we shall of course by-pass difficulties arising from translation, but we are still left with the problem of finding the meaning that the original writers intended to convey. Since most of us use a translation of the Bible our search for the meaning of doubtful words should begin by finding the original Hebrew or Greek words used. Fortunately we do not need to be linguists[1] because there exist excellent concordances and Bible word-books which provide this information. Each concordance or word-book

---

1. In his preface Young wrote that his concordance was *"designed to lead the simplest reader to a more correct understanding of the common English Bible ..."*.

is based on one particular translation - in English most are based on the KJV e.g. Young's and Strong's concordances, William Wilson's *Old Testament Word Studies* and Vine's *Expository Dictionary of New Testament Words*. By looking up any English word used in the KJV we can discover the original Hebrew or Greek word used. Then by looking up that Hebrew or Greek word in the index we can discover all the different English words into which it has been translated in the KJV. In this way we can find all the Bible passages in which a particular Hebrew or Greek word was used, and by comparing the different usages we can usually arrive at a reasonably firm conclusion regarding the meaning intended by the writer.[1]

In searching for the meaning of Bible words it will soon be apparent that there is an interesting difference between Hebrew and Greek. Greek has a rich vocabulary with different words to convey different shades of meaning whereas Hebrew has a relatively small vocabulary with many unspecialized words having more than one meaning. For example, the Hebrew 'ben' which means 'offspring' is used for son, grandson, great-grandson or any descendant, and it is also applied to the progeny of animals. *Elohim*, a Hebrew word for 'God', also means 'gods' or 'idols' and occasionally 'judges' (see John 10:34-36).

'For ever'

A simple example of a Hebrew word with more than one meaning and which can only be understood in relation to the context is the word *ōlam* which means 'age' and with a preposition is translated 'for ever' or 'everlasting'.

In most cases this translation conveys the wrong meaning because it suggests 'without ending', whereas it really means 'age-lasting' or 'a long

---

1. Davidson, in his *Theology of the Old Testament* expressed it succinctly: 'Usage is the only safe guide, the concordance is always a safer companion than the lexicon'.

time' or, to use our own idiom, 'ages'. The length of time implied depends entirely on the context and is often conditional as in 1 Sam. 2:30:

> **Therefore the LORD God of Israel says: 'I said indeed that your house, and the house of your father, would walk before me *for ever*.' But now the LORD says: 'Far be it from me; for those who honour me I will honour, and those who despise me shall be lightly esteemed...'**

Another example of the limited duration of 'for ever' is found in Isa. 32:14-15 where, concerning Israel, Isaiah proclaims that "the hill and the watchtower will become dens *for ever*, the joy of wild asses, a pasture for flocks; *until* a spirit from on high is poured out on us ..."

In 2 Chr. 10:7 Rehoboam was advised by his older counsellors that if he spoke kindly to his people they would be his servants for ever. In this context 'for ever' obviously meant for as long as he reigned.

In 1 Sam. 1:22 Hannah dedicated her son to the LORD with the promise that she would "bring him that he may appear before the LORD, and remain there *for ever*". In this context, 'for ever' meant for the lifetime of Samuel, as indicated by his mother when she later proclaimed, "As long as he lives he shall be lent to the LORD." (v.28)

On the other hand, when used in relation to God, 'for ever' and 'everlasting' usually imply never-ending time as in Psa. 9:7, "But the LORD shall endure for ever". In many cases where eternity is intended the word is repeated, as in Psa. 10:16, "The LORD is king for ever and ever", or in Psa. 90:2, "... from everlasting to everlasting, thou art God".

An interesting example of the use of 'for ever' is found in 2 Sam. 7:12-17 where David was promised that his seed (Solomon) would occupy his throne and that his throne (dynasty) would last for ever. When applied to Solomon this promise was conditional. David clearly understood this when he repeated the promise to Solomon in these words, "I will establish his kingdom for ever *if he is steadfast to observe my commandments ...*" (1 Chr. 28:7). However, it is clear from Heb. 1:5, which quotes from 2 Sam. 7:14, that this promise to David had a second and greater fulfilment in David's greater son, the Lord Jesus Christ. So in its application to Christ, 'for ever' is unconditional; it is the time span when Jesus will occupy the throne of David for 1000 years (Rev. 20:6). A very important O.T. example of the use of 'for ever' will be considered when discussing the tree of life in Ch. 13.

In the N.T. the Greek *aiōn* has the same basic meaning as the Heb. *ōlam* i.e. age or age-lasting, the duration being determined by the context. So when Jesus promised his disciples that the Holy Spirit would remain with them for ever (John 14:16), it was for their lifetime. On the other hand, when Jesus promised that his followers would have 'everlasting life in the world to come' (Luke 18:30) he was clearly referring to life without end.

However in many N.T. passages, especially in the writings of John, *aiōios* is used to denote a way of life or quality of life rather than duration of life:

> ... that you may know that you have eternal *(aiōion)* life .... 1 John 5:13

> Whoever eats my flesh and drinks my blood has eternal life *(zōēn aiōnion)*, and I will raise him up at the last day. John 6:54

The *'aiōnion* life' is therefore a present experience as well as a hope of life without end after being raised at the last day.

When Jesus said, "He that believes in me has eternal life", it is sometimes claimed that never-ending life is an absolute certainty for the followers of Jesus. But *aiōnion* life does not necessarily mean never-ending life. The duration of our eternal life will depend on our faithfulness. God's faithfulness is an absolute certainty but we can never be certain of ourselves. The apostle Paul makes this clear in 1 Cor. 9:27,

> **But I keep under my body, and bring it into subjection: lest that by any means, when I have preached to others, I myself should be a castaway.**
>
> **KJV**

Here the inspired Apostle Paul touched on the inescapable fact that, notwithstanding all he had done for his Lord, there remained the possibility that he could fail. And so he wrote to Titus that he lived "in *hope* of eternal life which God, who cannot lie, promised before the world began." (Titus 1:2).

In the word studies which follow we shall deal only with a few passages where fundamental truths have been distorted by the misinterpretation of words.

CHAPTER 3

"IN THE IMAGE OF GOD HE CREATED HIM"

In Gen. 1 man is described as being made in the image (Heb. *tselem*) of God. Here is another word that has to be interpreted. Although it normally refers to physical nature, as in Gen. 5:3 where Adam begat Seth 'after his image', we need to interpret the word differently in Gen. 1 because man was formed of dust of the ground, i.e. the elements of the earth. Anatomically he closely resembles the higher apes. In fact there are no organs or structures in the human body which are not represented in the bodies of the higher apes. Man therefore does not possess any unique *bodily* features which can justify the idea that he was made in the physical image of God or the angels.

Admittedly angels in the Bible often appeared in human form, and on occasions were thought to be human. But these manifestations were clearly miraculous. When Manoah's wife was visited by an angel she could tell from his countenance that he was 'an angel of God, very terrible'. She also calls him 'the man' and later this man/angel is described as 'ascending in the flame of the altar' (Judg. 13:20) — showing that the angel was an immaterial being.

'Image' in Gen. 1:26 is clearly a metaphor for divine character; it refers to the special creation of man with the faculties of self consciousness, God consciousness, time consciousness, and of understanding abstract concepts such as good and evil.

Language, speech and writing are the 'nervous system' of our 'image'. From the beginning God is introduced as one who speaks - God said, "Let there be light". Our ability to comprehend and respond to the word of God is that which links us to God and enables us to strive to be fully 'in His image'.

The New Testament also uses 'image' as a metaphor for character. Thus in Col. 1:15 Jesus is described as the 'image of the *invisible* God', and in

Col. 3:10 the new nature of the Christian involves being 'renewed in *knowledge* according to the image of Him who created him'. Moreover, in Rom. 1:23 there is a solemn warning against changing 'the glory of the incorruptible God into an image made like to corruptible man and birds and four-footed animals and creeping things'. While God was pleased to create man in His spiritual image, man tends to create gods in physical images!

What is morality?

Physically man is an animal and shares with animals the two basic instincts namely self-preservation and reproduction. These are essentially selfish instincts designed to preserve the individual and the race. Man has the same instincts but he is also endowed with higher faculties (p.1) which enable him to control his animal instincts in accordance with knowledge communicated by language. This is the moral dimension which distinguishes man from beast. As we shall see (Ch. 18), if man fails to control his animal instincts, he is no better than the other animals.

Since 'survival of the fittest' is a self-evident law of nature, selfishness is the driving force in the natural world and even when one animal dies for another it is only a manifestation of the instinct for survival of the race. So if man is no more than an animal, he is doomed to be the victim of his selfish genes. He will be powerless to control himself because all humanly devised mechanisms for control will be selfish. For this reason the essential basis for morality must lie outside ourselves; it must be a superhuman or divine revelation. Hence the paramount need for the Bible and our acceptance of the Bible as the inspired word of God. The Bible alone insists that the selfish or 'carnal mind' is the root of the problem of evil (Chs. 29-30) and that the only remedy is the 'crucifixion' of our animal nature (Ch. 38).

CHAPTER 4

"THE WHOLE CREATION GROANS"

> **For we know that the whole creation (Gk. *ktisis*) groans and labours with birth pangs together until now. Rom. 8:22**

This passage is often understood to mean that the whole of nature is under a curse because of Adam's sin. This is the so-called doctrine of 'original sin'. But we need to look at the Greek word *ktisis* which is translated creation or creature in the English N.T.

Ktisis can mean either the act of creation or that which is created. Thus in Rom. 1:20 it refers to the original act of God's creation:

> **Ever since the creation of the world his eternal power and divine nature, invisible though they are, have been understood and seen through the things he has made. So they are without excuse. NRSV**

A similar meaning is evident in Mark 10:6 where Jesus says,

> **But from the beginning of the creation, God made them male and female.**

Where *ktisis* refers to things created it may refer to a building, as in Heb. 9:11, to human laws (ordinances) as in 1 Pet. 2:13, or to creation in general as in Rom. 1:25 and 8:39. But in the majority of cases it is clear that the word refers to mankind as in Mark 16:15:

> **And he said to them, "Go into all the world and preach the gospel to every *creature*."**

and in Col. 1:23:

... provided that you continue securely established and steadfast in the faith, without shifting from the hope promised by the gospel that you heard, which has been proclaimed to every *creature* under heaven. **NRSV**

It has a similar special meaning in 2 Cor. 5:17, Gal. 6:15, Col. 1:15 and Heb. 4:13. In Rom. 8:18-23 Paul uses the word four times in connection with a discourse on suffering and deliverance from suffering.

> **18** For I reckon that the sufferings of this present time are not worthy to be compared with the glory which shall be revealed in us.
> **19** For the earnest expectation of the *creature* waiteth for the manifestation of the sons of God.
> **20** For the *creature* was made subject to vanity, not willingly, but by reason of him who hath subjected the same in hope,
> **21** Because the *creature* itself also shall be delivered from the bondage of corruption into the glorious liberty of the children of God.
> **22** For we know that the whole *creation* groaneth and travaileth in pain together until now.
> **23** And not only they, but ourselves also, which have the firstfruits of the Spirit, even we ourselves groan within ourselves, eagerly waiting for the adoption, to wit, the redemption of our body. **KJV**

In this passage we have to decide whether Paul is speaking of God's creation in general or of man in particular. Since 'creature' in verses 19-21 is invested with human feelings it probably refers to mankind. Thus mankind waits with 'earnest expectation' and has been 'subjected in hope ... that it will be delivered'. It is often assumed however that the 'whole creation' in verse 22 refers to creation in general rather than to mankind. This verse is then used to underpin the thesis that the whole of creation was cursed as a result of man's sin.

But if we look at verses 22 and 23 together we see that there are two groups who are groaning and labouring. We suggest that 'creation' in verse 22 refers to mankind in general and verse 23 refers to the early Christians in particular. A legitimate translation of these verses would read "We know that the whole of mankind has been groaning in travail together until now, and not only mankind in general, but we ourselves, who have the firstfruits of the Spirit, groan inwardly as we wait for adoption as sons ...".

Since the Greek word *ktisis* can mean creation in general or mankind in particular then the translation of *ktisis* by the word 'creation' in verse 22 is an interpretation and therefore cannot be used to prove the theory that God cursed the whole of His creation because of man's sin. We shall be dealing with this theory in greater detail in Ch.13.

CHAPTER 5

"IN SORROW THOU SHALT BRING FORTH CHILDREN"

In pronouncing the punishment for her disobedience, God said to Eve,

> I will greatly multiply thy sorrow and thy conception; in sorrow thou shalt bring forth children; and thy desire shall be to thy husband, and he shall rule over thee. Gen. 3:16 KJV

It has been assumed that 'sorrow' means pain, so the NRSV has: "I will greatly increase your pangs in childbearing; in pain you shall bring forth children ...". A similar translation is found in most other versions including the NIV and NKJV. The Jerusalem Bible even has: "I shall give you intense pain in childbearing, you will give birth to your children in pain."

There are, however, two closely related Hebrew words translated by sorrow in the KJV of Gen. 3:16. 'Multiply thy *sorrow*' (Heb. *itstsabōn*) and 'in *sorrow* (Heb. *etseb*) thou shalt bring forth children'.

As always, the best way to determine the meaning of Bible words is to study their use in other contexts where the meaning is clear. *Itstsabon* is used in the next verse: "Cursed is the ground for thy sake; in *sorrow* shalt thou eat of it all the days of thy life." The only other occurrence of this word in the Bible is in Gen. 5:29 where it is translated 'toil'.

> ... he named him Noah, saying, "Out of the ground that the LORD has cursed this one shall bring us relief from our work and from the *toil* of our hands." NRSV

It will therefore be clear that the correct translation of *itstsabōn*, **as used in Genesis**, is *toil* or *labour*.

With regard to *etseb*, this is used in only five other places in the Bible, namely Psa. 127:2 and Prov. 10:22 where it is translated '*sorrow*', in Prov. 5:10 and 14:23 where it is translated '*labour*', and in Prov. 15:1 where it is used adjectivally as 'grievous'. In none of these contexts is there any suggestion that *etseb* means pain, so there is little justification for this translation in Gen. 3:16 and there are good reasons for accepting the REB translation which reads:

> **I shall give you great labour in childbearing;**
> **with labour you will bear children.**

Thus it is appropriate that the hard work involved in Eve's primary rôle in bearing children[1] should correspond to the hard work imposed on Adam in his rôle as the provider of food from the land.

This misunderstanding of words in Gen. 3:16 might not appear very important but it has had tragic consequences for countless women. It has led to the belief that labour pains are a punishment on women for Eve's disobedience and for centuries pain relief was forbidden in labour. In 1591 a lady of rank, Eufame Macalyane, sought the assistance of Agnes Sampson for relief of pain at the time of the birth of her two sons. Agnes Sampson was tried before King James, and for her heresy was condemned as a witch and was burnt alive on the castle hill of Edinburgh. It is ironic that the translation of Gen. 3:16 in the King James Version is not far from the truth, and if King James had studied the similar translation in his own Bishops' Bible he would have found no reason for condemning Agnes Sampson.

---

1. The Hebrew word *heron* which has been translated 'conception' in Gen. 3:16 is not found elsewhere in the Bible. But when the Hebrew Bible was translated into Greek in the 3rd century BC *heron* was translated *stenagmos* which means 'groaning' or 'sighing'. There is therefore some evidence for the NEB rendering of Gen. 3:16, "I will increase you labour and your groaning, and in labour you shall bear children".

It is a sad reflection on male attitudes to women that there has never been any suggestion that it would be wrong for men to use labour-saving implements to alleviate the hard labour to which Adam was condemned!

No attempt is being made to argue that childbirth is or should be painless, but there can be no doubt that the erroneous church doctrine that pain in childbirth is a divinely-ordained punishment on women has significantly contributed to human suffering, both by 'conditioning' women to feel severe pain and by discouraging attempts to make childbirth easier.

The misinterpretation of Gen. 3:16 has prejudiced the translation of other Bible references to childbirth. For example, in John 16:21 we read:

> **A woman when she is in travail has sorrow, because her hour is come: but as soon as she is delivered of the child she remembereth no more the anguish, for joy that a man is born into the world. KJV**

The Greek word translated anguish is *thlipsis* which is the ordinary Greek word for affliction or distress. We prefer the NJB translation:

> **A woman in childbirth suffers because her time has come; but when she has given birth to the child she forgets the suffering in her joy that a human being has been born into the world.**

While it is possible that God modified the physiology of human childbirth in response to sin, we believe that a careful reading of Gen. 3:16 suggests that the emphasis is on hard work rather than painful childbirth.

CHAPTER 6

THE 'WORD' (LOGOS) WAS MADE FLESH

> 1. In the beginning was the Word, and the Word was with God, and the Word was God.
> 2. The same was in the beginning with God.
> 3. All things were made by him; and without him was not anything made that was made.
> 4. In him was life; and the life was the light of men.
> 5. And the light shineth in darkness; and the darkness comprehended it not.   John 1:1-5   KJV

There has been much speculation on the meaning of the Greek word *logos* in this passage. Although *logos* is the ordinary Greek noun for 'word' it is evident that John is using it in a special way. *Logos* stands for something more; it is an example of metonymy (see Ch.22). The meaning of *logos* is extended to include the reason and intention behind the spoken word. So we read in 1 Pet. 3:15,

> .... be ready always to give an answer to every man that asketh you a reason *(logos)* of the hope that is in you ....   KJV

also in Acts 10:29,

> Therefore came I without gainsaying, as soon as I was sent for: I ask therefore for what intent *(logos)* you have sent for me.   KJV

John was writing to Greeks in their own language and using their own figure of speech. To a Greek philosopher *logos* was the mind of the god that controlled the universe and made order out of chaos. John took this Greek concept and showed how it found its true meaning in relation to God's creation in the beginning and to His special creation in His Son Jesus Christ.

There are clear echoes of Gen. 1 in John 1. The *logos* created all things (v.3) and brought light out of darkness (v.5). And in Genesis God spoke and light appeared. Each act of creation is prefaced by the statement, "And God said ...". God's word was invested with creative power. This is beautifully expressed in Psa. 33:6-9,

> By the *word* of the LORD the heavens were made, And all the host of them by the breath of his mouth. He gathers the waters of the sea together as a heap; He lays up the deep in storehouses. Let all the earth fear the LORD; Let all the inhabitants of the world stand in awe of him. For he *spoke*, and it was done; He *commanded*, and it stood fast.

So John tells us that the *logos* became flesh; the purpose of God from the beginning became enshrined in the Son of God who manifested the glory of the only begotten of the Father full of grace and truth (v.14).

It is commonly assumed that the Word in John 1 means Jesus Christ and that he was the Creator who made all things. This interpretation has been fostered by the biased translation of the KJV and later versions which use the male pronoun 'him' for the noun 'word'. This is incorrect. Greek inanimate nouns may be masculine, feminine or neuter, but in English, inanimate nouns are neuter — with a few exceptions such as when speaking affectionately about a ship or car. So although *logos* is masculine in Greek, a correct English translation will use the neuter pronoun 'it' for 'word'.

Good Greek deserves to be translated into good English. For example, the Greek word for 'table' is feminine but in translating from Greek to English we would not say, "This is my table; *she* has many uses." So a better translation of John 1:1-4 would read,

> "In the beginning was the Word, and the Word was with God, and God was the Word. The same was in the beginning with God. All things were made by *it*, and without *it* was made nothing that was made. In *it* was life, and the life was the light of men ..."

This was the translation of Tyndale which was followed by the Great Bible, the Geneva Bible and the Bishops' Bible. The revisers of the Bishops' Bible, who produced the King James, or 'Authorised Version', introduced the masculine pronoun. With the exception of Samuel Sharpe's revision of the Authorised Version (1880), Benjamin Wilson's *Emphatic Diaglott* and the *Concordant Literal New Testament* by A.E. Knock, no later English translator has had the courage to revert to Tyndale's correct translation.[1]

The KJV translation of John 1:1-4 is clearly the result of theological bias. The assumption that the *logos* is Jesus is used to support the view that Jesus was the Creator in Gen. 1. Having decided that the *logos* is Jesus Christ, the translators have allowed their prejudice to influence their translation. Their use of the male pronoun is an *interpretation*.

Once we understand that the *logos* of John 1 is God's creative Spirit then John 1:14 becomes comprehensible. The "Word became flesh"; this happened when the Holy Spirit brought about the conception of Jesus Christ as described in Luke 1:35:

> The angel said to her, "The Holy Spirit will come upon you, and the power of the Most High will overshadow you; therefore the child to be born will be holy; he will be called Son of God." NRSV

Matt. 1:18-23 also describes the conception of Jesus Christ. But in nearly all English translations verse 18 commences with a mistranslation: "Now the *birth* of Jesus was as follows". The Greek word which has been translated 'birth' is *gennēsis* which means 'begettal' or 'birth'. However it is clear from the context that Matt. 1 is describing the *conception* of Jesus. This was recognized by Wycliff, the first English translator of the Bible, who renders it, "Forsoth the generacioun of Christ

---

1. In the French Bible *logos* is translated *Parole* which is a feminine noun. John 1:3 is correctly translated, "Toutes choses ont éte faites par *elle*, et rien de ce qui a éte fait n'a éte fait sans *elle*".

was thus ...". And Ferrar Fenton[1] has, "However, the origin of Jesus the Messiah was thus ..."

The allusions to Gen. 1 in John 1:1-4 are designed to show the parallel between the old creation by God and the new creation by Jesus Christ. This parallel is beautifully expressed by Paul in 2 Cor. 4:6, "For it is the God who said, 'Let *light* shine out of darkness', who has shone in our hearts to give the *light* of the knowledge of the glory of God in the face of Jesus Christ." Jesus, the Light of the world, fulfils the symbolism in Gen. 1:1-4. So John continues his discourse in verses 9-10:

> **That was the true Light which gives light to every man coming into the world. He was in the world and the world was made through him, and the world did not know him.**

The Greek word translated 'world' in this verse is *kosmos* which primarily means 'order' or 'arrangement'. *Kosmos* has a variety of extended meanings depending on the context. Thus it can mean the universe (Rom. 1:20), the earth (John 21:25), mankind (Matt. 5:14), or society — especially as it organizes itself without God (John 8:23). John is not saying that the physical world was made by Jesus Christ. The *Kosmos* in John 1:10 refers to the Jewish society into which Jesus was born. This *kosmos* was made *through* Jesus Christ in the sense that the Jewish law was the shadow of which Jesus was the substance (Heb. 10:1). The Jews had been appointed custodians of God's plan of salvation (John 4:22) and yet when confronted by Jesus they did not know him, for we read, "... the world *(kosmos)* knew him not. He came unto his own and his own received him not (vv.10-11)". We shall look at another Greek word translated 'worlds' in the next chapter.

---

1. Ferrar Fenton was a nineteenth century businessman who gave up the spare hours of a lifetime to produce the first complete Bible in modern English, published in 1903.

CHAPTER 7

"BY WHOM HE MADE THE WORLDS"

Another passage which is often erroneously used to prove that Jesus is God, the Creator of the Universe, is found in the first two verses of the Epistle to the Hebrews where the KJV reads:

> God, who at sundry times and in divers manners spake in time past unto the fathers by the prophets, Hath in these last days spoken unto us by his Son, whom he hath appointed heir of all things, by whom also he made the worlds.

First we should adopt the correct translation of the Greek preposition as used by the NKJV and other modern versions which read, "... *through* whom also He made the worlds". Then we should note that the word for 'worlds' in the Greek is *aiōnas* which means ages or eras. So the passage does not imply that Jesus was involved in the creation of the material world but rather that from the beginning Jesus Christ was at the centre of God's plan of salvation. The Lord Jesus alone gives meaning and significance to history (the 'ages'); his sacrifice was foreshadowed in Eden (Gen. 3:15), Abraham rejoiced to see his day (John 8:56) and the Law of Moses was but a tutor to bring men to Christ (Gal. 3:24).

Thus Jesus was the *appointed* heir of all things (Heb. 1:2) and it was by *inheritance* that he *obtained* a more excellent name than the angels (v.4). Each of the italicised words clearly demonstrates that after his resurrection Jesus was *given* a status which he had not possessed before.

Another passage which is claimed to prove that Jesus was the creator is found in Col. 1:15-16 where the KJV reads:

> 15 Who is the image of the invisible God, the firstborn of every creature:

> **16** For by him all things were created, that are in heaven, and that are in earth, visible and invisible, whether they be thrones, or dominions, or principalities, or powers: all things were created by him, and for him.

Before analysing this passage it is important that we should again correct the mistranslations of the Greek prepositions in the KJV and adopt a better translation which reads:

> **15 He is the image of the invisible God, the firstborn of all creation;**
> **16 for in him all things in heaven and earth were created, things visible and invisible, whether thrones or dominions or rulers or powers - all things have been created through him and for him. NRSV**

The interpretation of this passage depends on understanding the scriptural use of the three key words, *image*, *firstborn* and *creature*.

Image. We have already shown in ch. 3 that 'image' (Heb. *tselem*) can mean character rather than identity, as when God created man 'in the image of God' (Gen. 1:27). Similarly the Greek *eikōn* is used for character in 2 Cor. 3:18 where Paul says that we can be changed into the image of the Lord.

Firstborn. The clue to the meaning of firstborn is in the immediate context where, in v.18, Paul asserts that Christ is "the beginning, the *firstborn from the dead* ...". Paul is therefore referring, not to the first creation in Gen. 1 but to the new creation - the church of the firstborn (Heb. 12:23). Paul describes the Lord Jesus as the "firstfruits of those who have fallen asleep" (1 Cor. 15:20) and in Rom. 1:4 he says that Jesus Christ was "declared to be the Son of God ... by the resurrection from the dead." Jesus Christ was therefore the firstborn of all those who will be raised from the dead to newness of life in the kingdom of God.

In Rom. 8:29 we have a significant verse which confirms this interpretation of both image and firstborn.

> For whom he foreknew, he also predestined to be conformed to the image of his Son, that he (Jesus) might be the first-born among many brethren.

Creation. There is no justification for assuming that 'creation' in Col. 1:15 relates to the physical creation of Gen. 1. As we have shown (Ch.4) the Greek word for creation in verse 15 is *ktisis* which relates either to creation in general or to mankind in particular. In this context the next verse makes it clear that the reference is to mankind and relates to thrones, dominions, rulers and powers. In other words, Jesus Christ was at the centre of God's kingdom from the beginning of human time; he is the chief corner-stone of all ages; he is the focal point of God's cosmic purpose. The emphasis is on ruling authorities of which Jesus is supreme. Paul enlarges on this theme in Eph. 1:20-22 where he speaks of God's mighty power,

> Which he wrought in Christ, when he raised him from the dead, and set him at his own right hand in the heavenly places, Far above all principality, and power, and might, and dominion, and every name that is named, not only in this world, but also in that which is to come: And hath put all things under his feet, and gave him to be the head over all things to the church. KJV

It is clear from this passage in Ephesians (as also in Matt. 28:18) that Jesus was *given* this authority by God his Father. This is delegated authority and in the end Jesus will hand this authority back to his Father (1 Cor. 15:24-28).

The statement in Col. 1:16 that "in him were all things created" also finds a parallel in Ephesians where we read that God "created all things through Jesus Christ ... according to the eternal purpose which he accomplished in Christ Jesus our Lord" (Eph. 3:9,11). This passage makes it clear that the creation was through Jesus in the sense that Jesus was central to God's *purpose* and plan of salvation from the beginning of human time. This is evident from Rev. 13:8 where Jesus is described as the 'lamb slain from the foundation of the world' (*kosmos*). With His foreknowledge God could see Jesus on the cross from the beginning. For this reason God loved the Lord Jesus 'before the foundation of the world' (John 17:14) **and it is the infinite privilege of God's adopted sons to be 'chosen *in him* before the foundation of the world' (Eph. 1:4) and to inherit the kingdom prepared for them 'from the foundation of the world.' (Matt. 25:34)**

The verses we have been considering are expressions of God's foreknowledge. Our difficulties in understanding them relate to our time-bound nature. The inspired word of God speaks of a pre-existent Jesus because God sees the end from the beginning and so He speaks of things that are future in the past tense. Thus in commenting on the promises to Abraham given before the birth of Isaac, Paul writes that Abraham was called a father of many nations by God "*who gives life to the dead and calls those things which do not exist as though they did.*" (Rom. 4:17)

Calling things that are not, as though they existed, is a figure of speech known as prolepsis (see Ch. 32) and when used by inspired writers in relation to future events of which God alone had foreknowledge it is called the *prophetic perfect*.

So we see that from the beginning God created the heavens and the earth and that from the beginning God planned a new heavens and a new earth through his only begotten son Jesus Christ our Lord. In God's timeless dimension Jesus existed from the beginning. He is the alpha and omega, the beginning and the end of God's purpose (Rev. 1:8).

CHAPTER 8

"SON OF GOD"

> And the angel answered and said to her, "The Holy Spirit will come upon you, and the power of the Highest will overshadow you; therefore, also, that holy one who is to be born will be called the Son of God." Luke 1:35 NKJV

In our quest for an understanding of the divine nature of our Lord Jesus Christ we recognize that we are treading on holy ground and that this is a subject that should be approached with reverence and humility. In John 5:18 we read,

> Therefore the Jews sought the more to kill him, because he had not only broken the sabbath, but said also that God was his Father, making himself equal with God. KJV

Whatever the Jew meant by 'equal with God' Jesus made it abundantly clear in his reply that as the Son of God he was utterly dependent on his Father.

> ... The Son can do nothing of himself, but what he sees the Father do ... (v.19) KJV

In John 10:30 Jesus said, "I and my Father are one". By taking this literally the Jews accused Jesus of making himself God. Once again Jesus corrected their false reasoning by reminding the Jews that he had said that he was the Son of God and performed the works of his Father.

> Do you say of him whom the Father sanctified and sent into the world, 'You are blaspheming', because I said, 'I am the Son of God'? John 10:36

It is ironic that those who assert that Jesus is God are falling into the same error as those Jews who falsely accused Jesus of making himself God.

"I and my Father are one"

What exactly did Jesus mean when he claimed oneness or unity with his Father? Was he implying that he was the same person? We must not jump to this conclusion because oneness has different shades of meaning as is evident from John 17:20-22 where Jesus speaks of the unity of the Father and the Son *and* his disciples.

> Neither pray I for these alone, but for them also which shall believe on me through their word; That they all may be one; as thou, Father, art in me, and I in thee, that they also may be one in us: that the world may believe that thou hast sent me. And the glory which thou gavest me I have given them; that they may be one, even as we are one. KJV

This passage teaches that we can share the same kind of unity with Jesus as he shares with his Father. This is a unity of mind and purpose. Jesus never claimed identity with God. God was his Father and he was the Son of God. What does this word 'Son' really mean?

The Hebrew word *ben* and the Greek word *huios* both mean son or descendant however far removed. Thus Jesus is described as son of Mary (Matt. 1:25) and son of David and son of Abraham (Matt. 1:1).

The sonship of Jesus was unique in that he was both son of Mary and Son of God. Jesus frequently called himself 'son of man' referring to the fact that he was born of Mary and thereby inherited human nature with all its problems and temptations (Heb. 2:14-17). But Jesus also recognized his divine sonship at an early age as when he protested to his parents at the age of twelve, "Did you not know that I must be about my Father's business?" (Luke 2:49)

We are therefore drawn to the conclusion that if Jesus was *fully human* by inheritance from his mother he was likewise *fully divine* by inheritance from his Father. Unfortunately the balance of these relationships has been skewed by the trinitarian concept that Jesus is no less than God Himself. This idea changes the plain meaning of the word 'son'.[1]

But it is obvious that Jesus Christ's relationship to God his Father is not of the same essence as a man's relationship to his earthly father. Being fully man he had a human physical constitution. Being fully divine he had the *mind* of God.

As the Son of God, Jesus was specially endowed with the Holy Spirit of God. It was the Holy Spirit which brought about his conception (Greek: *gennēsis* in Matt. 1:18) and when he was baptized the Holy Spirit descended on him and a voice from heaven said, "You are my beloved Son; in you I am well pleased". Throughout his life Jesus continued to be guided by the Holy Spirit. Unlike many, who ignore or cast off parental advice when they become adults, Jesus remained in close communion with his Father so that he could say, "I do nothing of myself; but as my Father taught me I speak these things. And he who sent me is with me. The Father has not left me alone, for I always do those things that please him." (John 8:28)

---

1. If Jesus Christ's relationship to his Father is that of a son to a father then it is entirely appropriate that he inherits the names of God his Father. It is an almost universal custom that sons perpetuate the names of their fathers. Thus, in Isa. 9:6 the Messiah is called "Wonderful counsellor, Mighty God, Everlasting Father, Prince of Peace". Thomas rightly exclaims to the risen Lord, "My Lord and my God". And the writer to the Hebrews correctly applies the names of God in Psa. 45 to the Lord Jesus, "Your throne, O God, is for ever and ever; a sceptre of righteousness is the sceptre of your kingdom. You love righteousness and hate wickedness; Therefore God, your God, has anointed you with the oil of gladness more than your companions" (Heb. 1:8-9). From time immemorial sons have inherited the names of their fathers, and yet when Scripture gives Jesus the names of God it is assumed that Jesus and God must be the same person!

Not only did Jesus continue to receive advice from his Father but he also remained subject to Him, as emphasized by the writer to the Hebrews —

> ... **who, in the days of his flesh, when he had offered up prayers and supplications, with vehement cries and tears to him who was able to save him from death, and was heard because of his godly fear, though he was a Son, yet he learned obedience by the things which he suffered, and having been perfected, he became the author of eternal salvation to all who obey him.** Heb. 5:7-9

The supreme act of submission to the will of his Father was manifest in the garden of Gethsemane when Jesus pleaded with God saying, "O my Father, if it be possible, let this cup pass from me: nevertheless not as I will, but as thou wilt". (Matt. 26:39)

The agony in the garden of Gethsemane highlights what is perhaps the most serious objection to the concept of Jesus as 'God the Son'. If Jesus is God then there was no possibility that he could have failed in his struggle against the temptations arising from the human nature inherited from his mother. His temptations were real because he shared our weaknesses.

> **Inasmuch then as the children have partaken of flesh and blood, he himself likewise shared the same ... Therefore in all things he had to be made like his brethren, that he might be a merciful and faithful high priest in things pertaining to God, to make propitiation for the sins of the people. For in that he himself has suffered, being tempted, he is able to aid those who are tempted. Heb. 2:14-18**

It is ironic that those who believe that they are honouring Jesus by equating him with God are in fact dishonouring him; if Jesus were God, then his struggle against sin would have been a charade and his victory would have been a foregone conclusion. As it was, his victory over sin was a hard won battle. The outcome was a victory both for himself and for all those who obey him.

Son of God and son of man

As Son of man, Jesus grew up and matured under the discipline of his earthly parents. Luke tells us that a parallel growth and development took place in his relationship to his heavenly Father.[1]

> And the child grew and became strong in spirit, filled with wisdom; and the grace of God was upon him. ... Then he went down with them and came to Nazareth, and was subject to them, but his mother kept all these things in her heart. And Jesus increased in wisdom and stature, and in favour with God and men.
> Luke 2:40 & 51-52

After his baptism Jesus received a special blessing from his Father with the words, "You are my beloved Son; in you I am well pleased" (Matt. 3:17). This testimonial was repeated after the transfiguration (Matt. 17:5).

The resurrection of Jesus from the dead was the seal of God's approval. After his resurrection God invested Jesus with additional power and authority. Just before his ascension Jesus told his disciples, "All authority has been given to me in heaven and on earth." This authority was God's gift to His Son. It is **delegated** power; it was not his from the beginning nor will it always be his, as Paul states in 1 Cor. 15:27 where we read,

---

1. Readers familiar with historical theology will recognize that this view of the Son of God as a created being is the 'heresy' known as Arianism. But they will also know that the Nicene creed, with its statement that Jesus was 'of one substance with the Father' was the product of a long and often bitter debate between Athanasians and Arians and that it was not produced in its final form until the Council of Constantinople in 381 and was not declared official until the Council of Chalcedon in 451.

> For "He has put all things under his feet." But when He says "all things are put under Him", it is evident that He who put all things under Him is excepted. Now when all things are made subject to Him, then the Son Himself will also be subject to Him who put all things under Him, that God may be all in all.

This is a highly significant passage in which it is quite clear that the Son of God is *eternally* subject to his Father. It is often argued that the passages referring to Jesus Christ's dependence on God relate to his earthly existence and his human nature. But in this passage Paul makes it clear that the resurrected and glorified Son of God is still subject to the will of his Father.

This is also shown in Acts 4:29-30. Following their release by the Jewish authorities Peter and John gave thanks for their deliverance and asked for God's continued help in these words,

> And now, Lord, behold their threatenings: and grant unto thy servants, that with all boldness they may speak thy word. By stretching forth thine hand to heal; and that signs and wonders may be done by the name of thy holy child Jesus. KJV

'Child' in the Gk. is *pais* which by extension also means 'servant', as in Matt. 8:6. So Jesus, who has been given all authority in heaven and on earth (Matt. 28:18), is still the child and servant of God his Father.

CHAPTER 9

"IN MY FATHER'S HOUSE ARE MANY MANSIONS"

The above statement of Jesus' as translated in the KJV of John 14:2 is an important example of why we need to find the original meaning of Bible words by comparing Scripture with Scripture and by looking at the words in their context in the chapter and in the wider context of Scripture as a whole. These words are frequently quoted at funerals to comfort and assure the mourners that their loved ones have been taken up to be with God in heavenly 'mansions'. Consoling words, but are they true?

Consider first the expression, 'Father's house'. The literal meaning of this expression is easy to determine because Jesus used it in the same Gospel when in John 2:16 he rebuked those who had polluted the temple with the words, "Take these things out of here! Stop making my Father's house a market-place!" So 'Father's house' was the temple. But in John 14:2 Jesus was obviously referring to a spiritual house; in other words he was using the temple or 'Father's house' as a metaphor representing his followers. This is a common New Testament figure of speech and is used by Paul in 2 Cor. 6:16:

> **What agreement has the temple of God with idols? For we are the temple of the living God; as God said, "I will live in them and walk among them, and I will be their God, and they shall be my people." NRSV**

It is also used in Heb. 3:6 where we read,

> **Christ, however, was faithful over God's house as a son,** *and we are his house* **if we hold firm the confidence and the pride that belong to hope. NRSV**

Having determined that 'Father's house' is the body of believers we now look at the word 'mansions' and find that in the REB and NRSV it is translated 'dwelling places'. By using a concordance we quickly discover that the original Greek word is *monē* and that Jesus used the same word in the same discourse in verse 23 but in this case it has been translated 'abode' in the KJV, 'home' in the NKJV and 'dwelling' in the REV.

> **Those who love me will keep my word, and my Father will love them, and we will come to them and make our home with them. John 14:23   NRSV**

So we see that Jesus' assurance that "in my Father's house are many mansions" has nothing to do with going to heaven. It is an assurance by Jesus that there are many abiding places in the body of believers or Church of God. But why did the disciples need this reassurance? Why were they worried? The reason will be found in the previous chapter where in verse 33 he warns his disciples that he is going away to a place where they cannot come - referring to his ascension into heaven. This prospect must have been daunting to a band of followers who had abandoned their livelihoods to follow Jesus and expected him to deliver their country from the Roman power (Luke 24:21, Acts 1:6).

In the discourse which follows in John chapters 14, 15 and 16, Jesus reassures his followers that although he was going away he would return to them in the form of a Comforter or Helper, which was the Holy Spirit, and would provide for all their needs. So he continues in 14:3:

> **And if I go and prepare a place for you, I will come again and take you to myself, so that where I am, there you may be also.**

What did Jesus mean by saying that he would come again and be with them? The answer is given in verses 16 and 17:

> **And I will pray the Father, and he will give you another Helper, that he may *abide* with you for ever — the Spirit of truth, whom the world cannot receive, because it neither sees him nor knows Him; but you know Him, for He *dwells* with you and will be in you.**

With the help of our concordance we discover that the words 'abide' in verse 16 and 'dwell' in verse 17 are both *menō* in the original Greek. From this is derived the noun monē, translated 'mansions' or abiding places in verse 2. *So the promise of Jesus was that the Holy Spirit would come and find an abiding place in the hearts of his disciples.* That this is the theme of these chapters is evident from the fact that this promise is repeated over and over again in the same discourse (John 14:23-26; 15:26; 16:7, 13 and 16).[1]

This short study of a frequently misinterpreted passage demonstrates the importance of finding the original meaning of Bible words and how easily this can be accomplished by looking at the context and comparing Scripture with Scripture with the aid of a concordance. And it leads us to the important conclusion that, far from teaching that believers will be taken *up* into heavenly 'mansions', Jesus is reassuring his disciples that he will come *down* from heaven in the form of the Holy Spirit to make his abode with them and to guide them into all truth. This of course is exactly what happened on the day of Pentecost.

---

1. It would be a great mistake for the reader to suppose that we are casting any doubt on the personal return of Jesus Christ when we suggest that John 14:3 relates to the coming of Jesus in the form of the Holy Spirit Helper. Acts 1:11 declares emphatically and unequivocally that Jesus will return in a personal and bodily form. Moreover, *after* they had received the Holy Spirit the Apostles continued to proclaim the return of Jesus from heaven, as in Acts 3:21.

CHAPTER 10

ADULTERY AND FORNICATION

> "And I say to you, whoever divorces his wife, except for sexual immorality *(Gk. porneia)*, and marries another, commits adultery *(Gk. moicheia)*; and whoever marries her who is divorced commits adultery."
> Matt. 19:9

The various interpretations of the Greek word *porneia* in this passage and in Matt. 5:32 have resulted in endless controversy. Because the exceptive clause ('except for sexual immorality') is omitted in the parallel passage in Mark 10:11 and also in Luke 16:18 and Rom. 7:3, it is argued that the exceptive clause in Matthew is an interpolation and therefore marriage can never be dissolved. But there is no textual evidence for this theory. It is held by many higher critics who claim that Mark's record is the original and that the 'editor' of Matthew's gospel added the clause to please his Jewish readers. We do not accept this critical analysis because we believe that we have the inspired record of Matthew himself.

Others maintain that the exceptive clause in Matt. 19:9 was Christ's interpretation of the Law of Moses which only applied to his Jewish interlocutors and they argue that the statement in Mark 10:11, which omits the exceptive clause, was spoken to his disciples privately and was therefore the rule for Christians.[1] But the exceptive clause cannot be restricted in this way because in Matt. 5:32 it is part of the 'Sermon on the Mount' which is Christ's code of ethics for all time. Moreover, it is clear that the exceptive clause is not an exposition of the Law of Moses

---

1. Mark's reference in the next verse to a woman divorcing her husband relates to the fact that in later Jewish law a wife could obtain a Court Order forcing her husband to grant her a divorce. Therefore this verse does not support the theory that Mark was writing for Christians and Matthew for Jews.

because this prescribed the death penalty both for adultery and for a woman who was found not to be a virgin on her wedding night (see Deut. 22:13-30). There are therefore no good reasons for regarding the exceptive clause as either uninspired or irrelevant for Christians.

As we shall see in ch. 31, the omission of a word or words is a common figure of speech known as ellipsis, and the omission does not negate the existence or importance of the omitted words. We are therefore obliged to attempt to clarify what Jesus meant when he used the word porneia in Matt. 5:32 and 19:9. The Greek word *moicheia* is translated adultery and means precisely that; it is a specific term. On the other hand in N.T. Greek *porneia* is a generic term which covers a number of sexual vices, especially harlotry but also fornication (pre-marital unchastity), adultery and incest. The meaning will depend on the context.

When *porneia* is used in a list that includes *moicheia*, as in Matt. 15:19, then clearly it has a more restricted meaning and does not include adultery. It the passage under consideration however, it is not part of a list and there is no reason why *porneia* should not include adultery. Here are three examples where *porneia* includes adultery:

1. The Jews of Christ's day would be familiar with the use of porneia in their Greek O.T. In Hosea 2:2 they would read, "Plead with your mother ... let her put away her whoredoms *(porneia)* ... and her adulteries *(moicheia)*." Here *porneia* and *moicheia* are used in relation to the same married woman and the same acts.

2. In several passages such as 1 Cor. 6:18 and 1 Thes. 4:3 believers are commanded to abstain from *porneia* ('fornication' in the KJV). Surely this prohibition would include adultery as well as fornication, so the NKJV and NIV have 'sexual immorality'.

3. In 1 Cor. 5:1 Paul uses *porneia* to describe sexual union between a man and his stepmother, demonstrating that *porneia* can be applied to both adultery and incest. Again the NKJV has 'sexual immorality'.

Therefore since *porneia* can refer to any kind of sexual immorality we have to use our own judgement in deciding what kind of sexual immorality Jesus meant in the exceptive clause. Those who argue that Jesus was only referring to premarital unchastity must face the moral difficulty that this interpretation makes the deliberate breaking of solemn marriage vows less serious that a single act of fornication by someone who had made no vows. But because we cannot be dogmatic the revisers of the King James Bible translate *porneia* in Matt. 5:32 and 19:9 by 'sexual immorality' and it is translated 'unchastity' in the NRSV and 'marital unfaithfulness' in the NIV.

The Divine Ideal

The New Testament teaches that any unchastity, whether before or after marriage, is sinful. Jesus said, "He which made them at the beginning made them male and female ... For this cause shall a man leave his father and mother and shall cleave to his wife and they twain shall be one flesh ... what therefore God hath joined together let not man put asunder." Paul tells us that a Christian marriage symbolizes the union of Christ — the Bridegroom, and the Church — his bride. It is therefore a holy union which should not be broken.

However, we are all sinners and inevitably some marriages will break down. At such times we look to the Scriptures for guidance. Hosea 3:1 teaches us that we should follow God's example and extend forgiveness to an unfaithful partner. Jesus said our forgiveness must be unlimited — 'until seventy times seven' (Matt. 18:22). The fact that Jesus allowed divorce does not mean that he advised it. But forgiveness can only bear fruit when there is repentance. Persistent and **unrepented** unfaithfulness means that the man and his wife are no longer 'one flesh' and they cease to be a symbol of the unity of the church. Those who deny the possibility of divorce in such cases are perpetuating a situation which is a travesty of the spiritual symbology of marriage.

Some of those who recognize the futility of maintaining an irretrievably broken marriage argue that although divorce can be allowed it should not be followed by remarriage. They quote 1 Cor. 7:10-11 in support:

> "And unto the married I command, yet not I, but the Lord, Let not the wife depart from he husband: but if she depart, let her remain unmarried, or be reconciled to her husband: and let not the husband put away his wife." KJV

Here Paul is dealing with a wife who had left her husband. Paul advises her not to remarry and the husband not to divorce her because this would prevent reconciliation. Adultery is not mentioned and we should not assume that either the wife or husband was guilty of adultery. There is therefore no justification for arguing that this passage supports the idea that the innocent party to a divorce on the grounds of adultery cannot remarry. This theory is contrary to all we know concerning Jewish customs in the time of our Lord when divorce automatically conferred the right to remarry.

A common objection to divorce for any reason is a quotation from Mal. 2:16, *"the LORD ... hateth putting away"*. This is a classic example of quoting out of context. Here Malachi was referring to the nation of Israel as a man who had *"dealt treacherously against the wife of his youth"*. The 'wife of his youth' was the covenant which had been broken (v.14). Israel's treachery has no relevance to divorce for adultery because such a divorce would have been legal and therefore could not have been described as treacherous.

No attempt has been made to explore all the ramifications of the complex subject of divorce and remarriage. All we have sought to establish is that the meaning of a single Greek word *porneia* is essential for a fruitful discussion, and the search for its meaning reveals that there are areas of this subject where we should not be dogmatic. Every case must be judged on its merits. Understanding, compassion and forgiveness must be paramount.

Conclusion

We have chosen a few examples to show the importance of determining the meaning of Bible words by allowing the Bible to interpret itself. But words do not stand on their own; they are building-blocks for constructing phrases, sentences, paragraphs, chapters and books. The meaning of words often depends on the way they are built into phrases and sentences. When words are arranged or used in other than a straightforward way, we call these constructions figures of speech. These will be considered in the next section.

PART 2

FIGURES OF SPEECH

CHAPTER 11

When words are assembled into phrases we find that there may be several ways of saying the same thing. Language is flexible and often subtle, and words can be woven into many different figures of speech such as idiom, metaphor, hyperbole, irony, personification, etc.

Figures of speech are often more effective than plain words in conveying meaning. But there is a danger that if the figure of speech is not recognized it could lead to misunderstanding. The Bible is rich in figurative language, especially in the poetical books and in the Gospels. We shall deal in detail with only those figures of speech which have led to difficulties in translation or important differences in understanding.

IDIOM

An idiom is a peculiarity of phraseology approved by usage and sometimes having a meaning other than its logical or grammatical one. All languages are idiomatic because words and phrases readily acquire special meanings. A common archaic English idiom found throughout the KJV Bible is the expression 'it came to pass' which approximately means 'and'.

A typical N.T. idiom is found in John 18:37 where Pilate asks Jesus whether he is a king. Jesus replies, "You say that I am a king", meaning, "You say truly that I am a king." This idiom expresses strong affirmation and should not be misunderstood because we have a similar but less solemn idiom in English when we make the affirmation, "You've said it" or "You can say that again!".

However, most idioms are peculiar to one group of people or country and often present problems for translators. Hebrew is a highly idiomatic language and since the Jewish writers of the New Testament, as well as Jesus himself, were familiar with the Hebrew Old Testament, we find many Hebrew OT idioms carried over into the Greek of the New Testament. Thus in the KJV quotation of Psa. 95:11 in Heb. 4:3 we read:

> **As I have sworn in my wrath, if they shall enter into my rest.**

This is a Hebraistic negative which means "They shall not enter into my rest." The writer to the Hebrews transferred the idiom into Greek because he knew his Jewish readers would understand it. The KJV translators then transferred the same idiom into English. But for those unfamiliar with the Hebrew idiom this could lead to difficulties, and so the RV and later translators have changed the KJV "if they shall enter into my rest" to "They shall not enter into my rest."

Unfortunately the subtleties of many idioms are not translatable. For example, Jesus in Gethsemane prays to God, "My Father, if it is possible, let this cup pass from me; yet not what I want but what you want." Those unfamiliar with Hebrew idioms might think that Jesus was praying for something which he knew could not be. However, stating something which is wrong or cannot be, and then rejecting it afterwards, is idiomatic (epitrophe). Another example is found in Eccl. 11:9:

> **Follow the inclination of your heart and the desire of your eyes, but know that for all these things God will bring you into judgement. NRSV**

A particularly difficult idiom for translators is the Hebrew expression 'one that pisseth against the wall'. This obviously refers to males but only in a pejorative sense. Thus in the KJV of 1 Sam. 25:22 we read, "So and more also do God unto the enemies of David, if I leave of all that pertain to him by the morning light any that pisseth against the wall". The RSV and NKJV translate the idiom by a single word, 'male'. But this illustrates the risk of losing subtle meaning in translating idioms. The word 'male' loses the derogatory overtone, so we find the Jerusalem Bible translators attempting to restore the loss by using 'manjack'. In contrast to this harsh idiom for males, many idioms are refinements or euphemisms. For example, to 'cover the feet', as in 1 Sam. 24:3, means to squat and defecate. In the next five chapters we shall deal with some idioms that have doctrinal implications.

CHAPTER 12

KNOWLEDGE OF GOOD AND EVIL

A commonly misunderstood idiom is found in Gen. 2:17 and 3:5 where Adam and Eve were forbidden to eat of the tree of knowledge of good and evil. They were tempted to do so by the promise of the serpent, "God knows that when you eat of it your eyes will be opened, and you will be like God, knowing good and evil."

It is often assumed that prior to eating the forbidden fruit man was in a state of primeval innocence in which he was unaware of the existence of right and wrong. But if this were the case how would Adam have understood the prohibition and the importance of obedience to God's command? Moreover, if man was created amoral then he would be no better than natural beasts who have no moral perception and would not be subject to judgement.

From the beginning man was created in the image of God (Ch.3) which meant that he must have been equipped with the ability to distinguish between right and wrong. So although the expression 'knowledge of good and evil' implies innocence when applied to very young children (as in Deut. 1:39 and Isa. 7:16) or loss of faculty in old age (as in 2 Sam. 19:35) it clearly has another meaning when applied to responsible adults like Adam and Eve. We have a clue to this meaning in Isa. 5:20-21 where we read:

> "Woe to those who call evil good, and good evil; Who put darkness for light, and light for darkness; Who put bitter for sweet and sweet for bitter! Woe to those who are wise in their own eyes, And prudent in their own sight!"

Here we have the essence of Adam and Eve's transgression — they decided that they knew better than God. In deciding that it was right to eat of the tree of knowledge of good and evil they were being wise in their own eyes and setting themselves up as judges of what was right and wrong.

Thus, the serpent was not offering Eve the ability to distinguish between right and wrong but rather the authority to decide what was right and what was wrong. Calvin expressed it succinctly. He said that the tree of knowledge of good and evil was forbidden "not because God would have him stray like sheep without judgement and without choice; but that he might not seek to be wiser than became him, nor by trusting to his own understanding, cast off the yoke of God and constitute himself an arbiter and judge of good and evil."

Used in this idiomatic way 'knowledge of good and evil' means the authority to *judge* what is right and what is wrong. We have an example of this in 2 Sam. 14:17, when Joab sent a 'wise woman' to David to persuade him to release Absalom. In speaking to David she used these words:

> **The word of my lord the king will set me at rest; for my lord the king is like the angel of God to discern good and evil ....   NRSV**

Knowledge of good and evil is an example of a common near-Eastern and Biblical idiom called *merismus* in which the extremes are used to encompass the whole; thus in Isa. 44:6, when God says, "I am the first, and I am the last", we understand that God is the first and the last and everything in between. And when we are told in Gen. 19:11 that both 'small and great' confronted Lot, this does not mean that his opponents were a group of young lads and old men but that all males were involved. This very common idiom may not be evident in the English translation. For example, the Hebrew 'both Dan and Beersheba' is translated, 'from Dan to Beersheba' because the idiom means all the land from Dan in the north to Beersheba in the south. And when in Exod. 18:13 we read that Moses was sitting in judgement 'from morning until evening', this conceals the fact that in the Hebrew the phrase is 'both the morning and the evening'.

So the expression 'knowledge of good and evil' encompasses all shades of right and wrong, and the tree should be seen as representing the entire range of moral authority. Therein lay the subtilty of the temptation; Eve was being offered nothing less than Divine status and authority. Hence the words of the serpent, "When you eat of it your eyes will be opened and *you will be like God*, knowing good and evil."

By taking the fruit of the tree of knowledge of good and evil, Adam and Eve were grasping at divine status and authority. Where the 'first Adam' failed the 'last Adam' succeeded. Although Jesus had divine nature he did not grasp at equality with God. As Paul writes in Phil. 2:5-6,

> **Have this mind among yourselves, which you have in Christ Jesus, who, though he was in the form of God, did not count equality with God a thing to be grasped.**
> **RSV**

Thus we see the importance of a correct understanding of this idiomatic expression. It defines the essential nature of satanic evil which stems from man's rejection of God's authority as the sole judge of what is good and what is evil. A more detailed analysis of Satan and the devil will be found in chs. 29 and 30 which deal with personification.

CHAPTER 13

INFINITIVE ABSOLUTE

The infinitive absolute construction is a common Hebrew idiom used to express a certainty. In this idiom two forms of the same verb are used. For example, in Gen. 18:10, "I will surely return to you" is a correct translation of the Hebrew, 'returning I will return'. And when Jacob was shown the torn and blood-stained coat of many colours he exclaimed, "Joseph rending is rent in pieces" which the KJV correctly translates, "Joseph is without doubt rent in pieces". Other examples are found in Exod. 21:28 and 23:4, Deut. 7:26, 12:2 and 13:10 and in 1 Kin. 2:37.

The Tree of Life

Very significant examples of the infinitive absolute occur in Gen. 2:16-17 where we read:

> **16 And the LORD God commanded the man, saying, "Of every tree of the garden you may freely eat; 17 but of the tree of the knowledge of good and evil you shall not eat, for in the day that you eat of it you shall surely die."**

In the Hebrew it reads, "Of every tree of the garden *eating you shall eat*", which means that, with one exception, Adam was encouraged to eat of every tree so this would include the tree of life. It is significant that the same infinitive absolute idiom is used in the next verse when God warns Adam that in the day that he eats of the tree of knowledge of good and evil he will 'surely die'. The Heb. is *'dying you will die'* — an indication of the absolute certainty of the consequence.[1]

---

1. The warning *"in the day that you eat of it you shall surely die"* implies that this was a capital offence punishable by execution on that day. Adam and Eve were not executed; they were given a limited reprieve because God clothed them with skins - a symbol of the 'covering' of their sin through the sacrifice of the

Since Adam and Eve were allowed to eat of the tree of life, it would not have conferred immortality. This suggests that it preserved them from corruption. So long as they ate of the tree of life their bodies would not decay and they would not die. It gave them incorruptibility but not immortality. An incorruptible body does not die; an immortal body cannot die.

We should not assume that living 'for ever' meant never ending life. As we have seen in Ch. 2, 'for ever' in the Bible means for an indefinite time the duration of which can only be determined by the context. So in this case it could mean for as long as they continued eating of the tree of life.

When Adam and Eve sinned they were driven out of Eden, access to the tree of life was barred and they were then subject to the processes of ageing and disease common to all the animal kingdom. Thus we read in Gen. 3:22-24:

> **22 Then the LORD God said, "Behold, the man has become like one of us, to know good and evil. And now, lest he put out his hand and take also from the tree of life, and eat, and live forever" -
> 23 therefore the LORD God sent him out of the garden of Eden, to till the ground from which he was taken.**

Now that man had sinned by grasping at divine authority it was necessary to prevent him from putting out his hand and eating the fruit of the tree of life. The tree of life was not for sinners; it was to be preserved for those who overcame sin (Rev. 2:7). God alone possesses and bestows incorruptibility and immortality (1 Tim. 1:17 and 6:16). Only at the resurrection will men be given both incorruptibility and immortality, as Paul writes in 1 Cor. 15:53,

---

Lamb of God "slain from the foundation of the world" (Rev. 13:18).

> For this corruptible must put on incorruption, and this mortal must put on immortality.[1]

There is no suggestion in Genesis 3 that Adam's sin brought about a change in his genetic make-up. The change that took place came as a result of his expulsion from Eden and being debarred from the tree of life. This meant that Adam's body then reverted to its natural state; his natural mortality was no longer held in abeyance. When he sinned he forfeited his right to partake of the tree of life.

The function of the tree of life as a preserver of life is demonstrated in Rev. 22:1-5 where we have a vision of Eden restored with a tree of life whose leaves are for the *healing* of the nations.

As we shall see, Adam was a representative man. The fact that Adam was allowed to eat of the tree of life and that after he sinned the tree was forbidden provides important clues about ourselves. We die because we sin and so have forfeited any right to the tree of life. Incorruptibility and immortality are gifts from God without which we perish:

> For the wages of sin is death; but the gift of God is eternal life through Jesus Christ our Lord. Rom. 6:23

We shall have more to say about the nature of our mortality in Ch. 16. Meanwhile we need to look at other consequences of the fall.

---

1. This is an example of Hebrew parallelism in the Gk. N.T. involving expansion (see poetry Ch. 33).

Other punishments of Genesis 3

In addition to the death sentence described in Gen. 3:19-24 Adam and Eve were given specific punishments which were related to their male and female roles.

We have already seen (Ch. 5) that the first part of Eve's punishment was the imposition of hard work in bearing children. In addition she was told that she would be subject to her husband's authority. This is not surprising when we recall that it was Eve who initiated the fall by enticing Adam to eat the forbidden fruit. It is relevant that Paul comments on this aspect of the fall in 1 Tim. 2:14.

With regard to the punishment of Adam, he was told that in future he would have to work very hard in order to survive.

> **... cursed is the ground because of you; in toil you shall eat of it all the days of your life; thorns and thistles it shall bring forth to you; and you shall eat the plants of the field. Gen. 3:17,18**

In future Adam would be faced with the natural world and there would be a constant struggle against weeds of the field. So they were driven from the garden of Eden into the world outside. The fact that the garden could be guarded by only one entrance at the east shows that it was an enclosed area, possibly a steep-sided valley. In this paradisal enclave Adam would be protected from hostile elements outside, although there was still work to be done because Adam was commanded to 'till and keep' the garden.

It is significant that a similar punishment was inflicted on Cain after he had murdered Abel,

> **"And now you are cursed from the ground ... When you till the ground, it will no longer yield to you its strength ..." Gen. 4:11,12**

Cain's punishment was that the area to which he was banished would not yield full crops. But in the case of Adam he was told that weeds (i.e. thorns and thistles) would be his particular problem.

Death in the natural world

It is often said that Rom. 5:12 teaches that Adam's sin not only resulted in his death but it also brought death into the animal kingdom. So it is argued that prior to the fall nature was vegetarian.

> **Therefore, just as through one man sin entered the world, and death through sin, and thus death spread to all men, because all sinned ...**

There is no suggestion in this verse that Paul is referring to animal death. On the contrary the logic of the argument is that death is the penalty imposed on sinful men. We all die because we all sin. Animals do not sin and suffer no penalty as a consequence.

One wonders whether those who postulate a deathless world before the fall have given serious thought to the radical changes required by this theory. Our world is not just a vegetarian world into which God has introduced some wild beasts such as wolves and lions! The whole ecology and balance of nature is based on a complex web of food chains so that it is true to say that in nature new life arises from death. Food chains are essential for life on earth for two reasons:

1. All plants and animals reproduce by producing far more seeds, eggs or offspring than are needed, so that a balance between species can only be maintained by the elimination of the excess by death at various stages of development.

2. Food chains recycle the earth's resources. For example, the excreta of birds that follow the plough give back to the soil the nutrients which have been obtained from soil grubs (beetles, centipedes, etc.) which have fed on protozoa and minute worms (enchytraeids) which have fed on bacteria and fungi which have fed on decaying plant life.

Anyone familiar with the biosphere and the operation of 'food chains' will know that the theory that sin brought animal death would necessitate a completely new creation after the fall. We have no evidence for this new creation in Gen. 3, nor do we have any evidence of a deathless creation in the fossil record.[1]

Relevant to the question of death before the fall is Gen. 1:30 which reads, "And to every beast of the earth, and to every bird of the air, and to everything that creeps on the earth, everything that has the breath of life, I have given every green plant for food."

This verse is often thought to teach that the original creation was deathless and entirely vegetarian. But there is another interpretation which reveals a fundamental truth about life on earth. In the oceans the basis of life is phytoplankton which consists of countless billions of free-floating minute photosynthesizing plants. These are eaten by minute animals called zooplankton and both kinds of plankton provide the food for all marine animal life. On the land, vegetation (photosynthesizing plants) provides the food for *all* terrestrial animals except those that live by fishing. So when a lion eats a deer it is consuming vegetation that has been processed in the stomach of the deer. *It will therefore be evident that the basis of all life on earth, whether on land, in sea or air, is plant life which derives its energy from the sun.* Thus Gen. 1:30 is expressing a profound biological truth — that all life depends on green plants. The essential lesson of Gen. 1:29,30 is surely that God has made the natural world self-sustaining.

---

1. Carnivorous animals are found throughout the fossil record. They include shark-like Devonian fish, dragon-flies and spiders in the Carboniferous, flesh-eating dinosaurs in the Mesozoic and sabre-toothed tigers in the Pleistocene, to name but a few. Those who believe that there was no death before the fall must therefore accept the theory that all the fossils were laid down following the fall in Eden (Ch. 36).

Of course we do not deny that God could have redesigned and recreated the living world as often as He wished. But in the absence of any compelling Biblical or scientific evidence, are we not justified in asking whether God would have inflicted disease and death on the whole animal kingdom because of our sins?

Augustinian 'original sin'

Augustine went much further. He taught that the sin of Adam and Eve alone brought disease and death and physical and moral depravity to all mankind. This view is difficult to reconcile with God's declared principles of justice.

A fundamental principle is that God does not punish men because of the sins of others. So important is this principle that a whole chapter (Ezekiel 18) is devoted to it; we read in verse 20:

> **The soul who sins shall die. The son shall not bear the guilt of the father, nor the father bear the guilt of the son.**

This principle was clearly stated in the law of Moses and was the reason why Amaziah did not slay the sons of Josiah (2 Chr. 25:4).[1]

> **The fathers shall not be put to death for their children, nor shall the children be put to death for their fathers; a person shall be put to death for his own sin.**
> **Deut 24:16**

If God does not punish children for the sins of their parents then would He have condemned all mankind because of one man's sin?

---

1. For an explanation of Exod. 20:5 which appears to contradict this principle, see Ellipsis (Ch. 31).

'In Adam' and 'in Christ'

We shall be returning to the subject of man's nature when considering the metaphorical use of 'flesh' in the New Testament (Ch. 18). Meanwhile we need to look at the second half of Rom. 5 because this is used to support the Augustinian teaching that our mortality and depravity are the result of Adam's sin alone. In verse 14 Paul says that Adam was a type of Christ and he then draws six contrasts between Adam and Christ which are summarized as follows:

15. By one man's offence many died
    - by one man, Jesus Christ, many receive grace.
16. Judgement from one brought condemnation.
    - the free gift brought justification.
17. By one man's offence death reigned
    - through one (Jesus Christ) the gift of righteousness reigns.
18. Through one man's sin all are condemned.
    - through one man's righteousness all are justified.
19. By one man's disobedience many were made sinners.
    - by one man's obedience many will be made righteous.
21. Sin reigned unto death.
    - grace reigned to eternal life.

These verses appear to teach that just as Adam brought death to all men so Jesus brings life to all. But Jesus made it clear that he only brings salvation to those who believe in him (Mark 16:16, John 14:6). So Paul's words are elliptical; the contrast is between Jesus who brings life to all who follow him and Adam who *introduced* death as a penalty for all who sin. Looking again at v.12 which introduces this section of Rom. 5 it is clear that Paul accepted that all men die *because*[1] all men are sinners.

---

1. The Greek *eph hō* is correctly translated 'because' in the NKJV.

> Therefore, just as through one man sin entered the world, and death through sin, and thus death spread to all men, because all sinned — Rom 5:12

When Adam sinned he suffered the consequences — he was expelled from Eden and deprived of the tree of life. Like Adam "we have all sinned and come short of the glory of God". For this reason the tree of life is still barred and remains out of reach until Eden is restored (Rev. 22:2). Adam was the first sinner and as a result the tree of life was barred but when Adam passed off the scene the Cherubim remained at the gate of Eden to guard the tree of life *because all have sinned*. Adam is the *representative* of all men; we each repeat the history of Eden and we each receive the 'wages of sin' which is death (Rom. 6:23). We are paid for what we do; we all sin, so we all die.

Just as Adam is the representative of the 'old man' so Jesus Christ is the representative of the new man. Jesus reversed Edenic history. He conquered temptation and by living a sinless life had a right to eat of the tree of life. So Paul wrote, "For as in Adam all die, even so in Christ shall all be made alive." This statement is elliptical[1]; Paul could mean "Because we all follow in the way of sinful Adam we all die, but all those who follow in the way of Christ will receive the gift of everlasting life".

A casual reading of Rom. 5:13-14 might appear to support the Augustinian theory that Adam's sin brought death by contaminating the whole race.

> **For until the law sin was in the world: but sin is not imputed when there is no law. Nevertheless death reigned from Adam to Moses, even over them that had not sinned after the similitude of Adam's transgression, who is the figure of him that was to come. KJV**

---

1. For an explanation of ellipsis see Ch. 31.

However, these verses cannot contradict the plain statement in the previous verse which teaches that all men die because all have sinned. The solution lies in understanding that Adam died because he was denied access to the tree of life. But Adam was not responsible for the fact that the tree of life remains barred to all mankind. It remains barred because we all sin, **even though we do not sin after the same manner as Adam**.

As Paul affirmed in Rom. 3:9-10 all men are 'under sin'; "there is none righteous no, not one". Sin is the 'sting of death' (1 Cor. 15:56) "and so death passed upon all men because all sinned". Immortality is the *gift* of God (Rom. 2:7) which will be bestowed at the second coming of Jesus Christ when he will grant access to the apocalyptic tree of life which bears twelve fruits (Rev. 22:2).

The problems imposed by the Augustinian doctrine of original sin have been the cause of much heart searching - so much so that one commentator on Rom. 5 wrote, "Unquestionably the mystery of the effects of the fall is extremely great and painful."[1] We suggest that if we accept that the effect of the fall was simply to deprive Adam of access to the tree of life then the painful doctrine of original sin will disappear. There is no need to postulate a change in man's human nature as a result of Adam's sin. Deprived of the tree of life, Adam's nature reverted to its original corruptible state. And since we are all sinners, we too have no access to the tree of life and we inherit Adam's corruptible nature. We are not condemned because of Adam's sin but because we follow his example.

This interpretation of the fall in Eden provides us with an alternative understanding of the so-called 'defilement' of the human race as a consequence of sin. It explains our nature as being the result of a loss of privilege rather than a positive change in our make up. **But both views reach the same conclusion which is far more important: we are all sinners and we are all in need of salvation from death.**

---

1. H.C.G. Moule. *Epistle to the Romans: Cambridge Bible for Schools and Colleges*, 1889, p.104.

CHAPTER 14

IDIOMS FOR THE SUPERLATIVE

There are three different idioms for expressing the superlative in Hebrew. A superlative may be expressed by joining a noun with its own plural in the genitive. Thus in Exod. 26:33 'Holy of Holies' in the Hebrew means most Holy, and 'Vanity of vanities' in Eccl. 1:2 means absolute vanity. Similarly, we have 'king of kings' in Dan. 2:37 and 'God of gods' in the Hebrew of Psa. 50:1.

Secondly, a superlative sense may be given to a word by connecting it with a divine name. Thus in Psa. 36:6 we have in the Hebrew, 'mountains of God' which has been correctly translated 'great mountains' in the KJV. In Gen. 30:8 'great wrestlings' is 'wrestlings of God' in the Hebrew, and in 1 Sam. 14:15 'great trembling' is 'trembling of God'.

Thirdly, we have the plural of excellence which first appears in Genesis 1 where Elohim is used as a name of the Creator. This is the plural form of Eloah (God) and literally means gods. But in Gen. 1 Elohim is followed by a singular verb and therefore refers to the one God who is above all other gods. This idiomatic use of the plural is also found in Prov. 30:3 where the Hebrew has 'holy ones' which means 'most holy'.

Although Elohim can mean angels, as in Psa. 8:5, this is practically never the case when it is the subject of a singular verb.[1] There is, therefore, no evidence in Gen. 1 for the idea that Creation was the work of angels. Nor is there any justification for the suggestion that Elohim refers to the Trinity.

---

1. See *Pentateuch and Haftorahs*, Ed. J.H. Hertz, Soncino Press, 1938, p.2. See also A.D. Norris - *What is His Name? A Study of Divine Titles*, Aletheia Press, BCM Box 175, London WC1N 3XX, 1986, pp 51-55.

In Gen. 1:26 we read:

> **And God said, Let us make man in our image, after our likeness: and let them have dominion over the fish of the sea, and over the fowl of the air, and over the cattle, and every creeping thing that creepeth upon the earth. KJV**

The use of the plural in "Let us make man in our image", is a Hebrew idiomatic way of expressing deliberation regarding an important decision, as in Gen. 11:7. God could have consulted with the angels concerning this most important aspect of His creation but the next verse reverts to the singular and makes it clear that God created man in *His* image (for the meaning of 'image' see Ch. 3.)

CHAPTER 15

COMPARATIVE NEGATIVE

Another common Bible idiom is the comparative negative in which something that is less important is negated by comparison with something which is much more important. So when Jesus says, in John 6:27, "Do not labour for the food which perishes, but for the food which endures to everlasting life ..." he is not saying that we should not work for our living but rather "Do not work as hard for perishable things as for eternal things."

Similarly in Luke 14:12 Jesus says, "when you give a luncheon or a dinner, do not invite your friends or your brothers or your relatives or rich neighbours ... but when you give a banquet invite the poor, the crippled, the lame and the blind." In other words it is more important to give hospitality to those who are deprived than to less needy relatives and friends. In Matt. 9:13 we read:

> **But go and learn what this means; 'I desire mercy, not sacrifice.' For I did not come to call the righteous but sinners to repentance.**

This is not a condemnation of sacrifices, nor is Jesus saying that God has no use for the righteous. The point is that since we are all sinners ('righteous' is ironical here) our greatest need is for God's forgiveness, and this depends not so much on our sacrifices (works) as on our repentance and our showing mercy to others.

'Not to baptize'

A failure to recognize this idiom has led to serious misunderstandings. For example, when Paul wrote in 1 Cor. 1:17, "For Christ did not send me to baptize, but to proclaim the gospel ..." he was not denying the importance of baptism - rather he was arguing that his first priority was to preach the gospel and that the identity of the baptizer was of no importance.

'Hate father and mother'

In Luke 14:26 Jesus says, "Whosoever comes to me and does not hate father and mother, wife and children, brothers and sisters, yes, and even life itself, cannot be my disciple." Jewish anti-Christian commentators accuse Jesus of contradicting the fifth commandment, that we should honour our parents. They fail to see that Jesus was dealing with priorities; the top priority is to honour God. So 'hate' is comparative and means 'love less'. This meaning is obvious when we consider that Jesus includes our own lives as the object of hatred.

Although a literal translation of Luke 14:26 will tell us exactly what Jesus said it can convey the wrong meaning to someone unfamiliar with the idiom. In such cases we can see an advantage in free translations such as the GNB which give the correct meaning to the words of Jesus, "Whoever comes to me cannot be my disciple unless he loves me more than he loves his father and his mother, his wife and his children, his brothers and his sisters and himself as well."

Does God care for oxen?

In 1 Cor. 9:9-10 Paul writes:

> **For it is written in the Law of Moses, Thou shalt not muzzle the ox when he treadeth out the corn. Is it for the oxen that God careth, or saith he it altogether for our sake? Yea, for our sake it was written: because he that ploweth ought to plow in hope, and he that thresheth, to thresh in hope of partaking. RV**

It appears that Paul is dismissing the idea that God cares for the welfare of oxen. However, if we examine the context we find that this cannot be so. In this chapter Paul is answering critics who accused him of reaping benefits from his preaching. In answer he puts forward the principle that a worker is entitled to benefit from his labours; thus the vinedresser eats the grapes and the shepherd partakes of the milk of his flock. He then points out that this principle is embodied in the Law of Moses where it is stated that the ox which is employed in threshing corn should not be muzzled but should be able to eat some of the corn. Later he uses exactly the same argument in 1 Tim. 5:17-18.

So when Paul appears to give a negative answer to the question, "Does God take care for oxen?" he is almost certainly using the comparative negative idiom. He is saying in effect, "Yes, although God cares for oxen, this law embodies a more fundamental and wide-ranging principle: that man's work should be appropriately rewarded" or as Jesus expressed it in Matt. 10:10, "The labourer is worthy of his food". Here is another example where a translator is justified in using paraphrase in order to avoid misunderstanding. This is done by Ferrar Fenton in his *Complete Bible in Modern English*:

> **For in the Law of Moses it is written: YOU SHALL NOT MUZZLE THE THRESHING BULLOCK. Bullocks are an object of care with God. But he speaks for us also, he wrote for us as well; because the ploughman ought to plough in hope, and the thresher ought to share in the hope.**

God's care for animals is evident from other Scriptures such as Exod. 23:12 where we learn that the sabbath rest was designed not only for man but also for working animals and Prov. 12:10 which reminds us that "a righteous man regards the life of his animal."

'Not against flesh and blood'

In Ephesians 6:12 Paul writes:

> For we do not wrestle against flesh and blood, but against principalities, against powers, against the rulers of the darkness of this age, against spiritual hosts of wickedness in the heavenly places.

'Flesh and blood' is a N.T. metonymy for human beings (Matt. 16:17, Gal. 1:16) or human nature (1 Cor. 15:50, Heb. 2:14). Paul was not telling the Ephesians that they did not have to wrestle against human opposition. He was using the comparative negative idiom. He was warning the Ephesians that their struggle was *not only* a battle against ordinary humans; they also had to contend with the powerful political enemies of their infant church - enemies that had already made him a prisoner in chains (Eph. 6:20).

What did Paul mean by 'high places' (Gk. *epouranios*). This word usually refers to the divine realm as in Eph. 1:3 and 20, but in the same epistle Paul used it as a metaphor for the ruling powers and expresses the hope that the gospel might reach even to them.

> ... to the intent that now the manifold wisdom of God might be made known by the church to the principalities and powers in the heavenly places.
> **Eph. 3:10**

So it is a reasonable assumption that in Eph. 6:12 *epouranios* also refers to the hostile ruling powers. There is therefore no need to interpret this passage as referring to a celestial conflict between good and evil.[1] This concept of dualism will be dealt with in Ch. 30.

---

1. The GNB in Eph. 6:12 has: *"For we are not fighting against human beings but against the wicked spiritual forces in the heavenly world, the rulers, authorities and cosmic powers of this dark age".* This is a paraphrase which not only fails to detect the comparative negative idiom but also fails to appreciate the Biblical use of 'flesh' as a metaphor for human nature (see Ch.18).

'Not with braided hair ...'

Another example of the comparative negative is found in 1 Tim. 2:9-10:

> **... in like manner also, that the women adorn themselves in modest apparel, with propriety and moderation, not with braided hair or gold or pearls or costly clothing but, which is proper for women professing godliness, with good works."**

Contrary to the Puritan ethic this passage does not condemn all forms of female adornment. Paul is saying, "Dress modestly; good deeds are more important than good looks".

An interesting example occurs in the words of the Samaritans to the woman who had met Jesus at Jacob's well. They said,

> **"Now we believe, not because of thy saying: for we have heard him ourselves, and know that this is indeed the Christ, the Saviour of the world." John 4:42 KJV**

The Samaritans were not dismissing the testimony of the woman; they were saying, "Now that we have seen the Christ we have more convincing evidence."

Other examples of the comparative negative idiom are found in Matt. 10:28, Luke 10:20 and 1 Pet. 3:21.

CHAPTER 16

Emphatic "Today"

This idiom consists of adding the adverb 'today' or 'this day' to a verb which introduces a solemn statement - the verb being one of declaration, testification, command or oath. It has the effect of enhancing the solemnity and importance of the statement.

The emphatic 'today' is a common idiom in both Hebrew and Aramaic, the two Semitic languages in which the Old Testament was written. There are some 70 occurrences of this idiom, of which 42 are found in the book of Deuteronomy where, for example, we read:

> **I call heaven and earth to witness against you *this day*, that you will soon utterly perish from the land which you cross over the Jordan to possess; you will not prolong your days in it, but will be utterly destroyed: Deut. 4:26**

This solemn warning is repeated:

> **If you do forget the LORD your God and go after other gods, serving them and bowing down to them, I give you a solemn warning *this day* that you will certainly be destroyed. Deut. 8:19 REB**

The Penitent Thief

In his response to the penitent thief on the cross Jesus used this idiom but nearly all translators have failed to appreciate it. This has led to a serious misunderstanding of the solemn promise which Jesus made to the thief in Luke 23:43 which should read:

> **Truly, I say to you *this day*, you will be with me in Paradise.**

We know that Aramaic was the native language of the Lord Jesus Christ because on occasions the Gospel writers give us his untranslated words as in Mark 5:41:

> **Then he took the child by the hand, and said to her, "Talitha cumi", which is translated, "Little girl, I say to you, arise."**

We also know that Jesus often quoted from Deuteronomy and all his answers to the temptations in the wilderness were taken from it.

There is no doubt that when Jesus was on the cross he spoke Aramaic because one of his last sayings is recorded untranslated by both Matthew and Mark. His cry, "Eli, Eli, lama sabachthani?" (My God, my God why have you forsaken me?) is the Aramaic form of the words of Psa. 22:1. So it is almost certain that in his reply to the thief Jesus would have used the idiom which was common to both his own native Aramaic and the Hebrew of the Old Testament - especially the book of Deuteronomy.

A correct translation of the promise to the thief should reproduce the true sense of the Aramaic. We find this in the earliest translation of the Greek New Testament into another language - the language of Palestine's nearest neighbour, Syria. Syriac is a dialect of Aramaic. In one of the oldest Syriac manuscripts of the Gospels (5th century Curetonianus) the translator has clearly recognized the idiom and translated the passage, "Amen say I to you today that with me you will be in the garden of Eden." By introducing the word 'that', which is not in the original Greek, the translator removed the need for any punctuation to determine the sense. *We therefore have the endorsement of an ancient and authoritative translation which precedes all the English versions by hundreds of years.*

A correct understanding of this passage is vitally important because the alternative translation completely distorts the message and introduces a serious contradiction. If Jesus said, "Truly, I say to you, Today you will be with me in Paradise", then he is promising the thief that they would both be in paradise on the day of their crucifixion and death. This cannot be true because elsewhere Jesus had emphatically declared that the sign of his Messiahship would be the fact that he would be "three days and three nights in the heart of the earth" (Matt. 12:40). Clearly Jesus could not have been in paradise and in the heart of the earth at the same time. It should be emphasized that there is no punctuation in the original Greek manuscripts of the New Testament (Fig. 1). Nor are there any spaces between the words, so if we were to transcribe the passage it would appear thus:

"TRULYISAYUNTOYOUTODAYYOUWILLBEWITHMEINPARADISE"

Fig. 1 shows the passage as it appears in the Codex Alexandrinus - one of the oldest Greek manuscripts of the complete Bible.

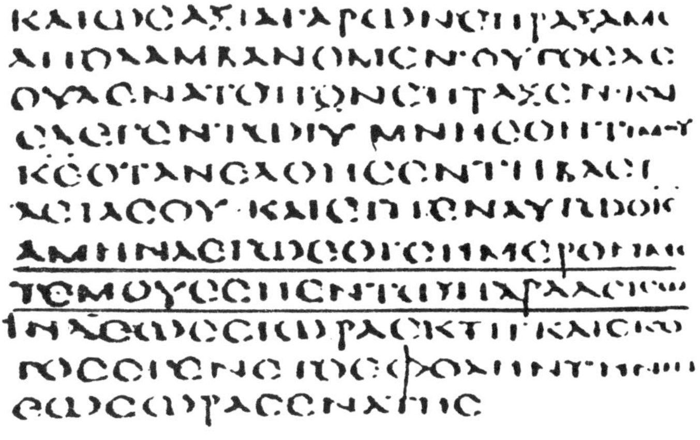

Fig. 1 Luke 23:43 in Codex Alexandrinus

All punctuation is an addition to the original text and reflects the opinion of the translator. The Greek adverb, 'today', *sēmeron*, can apply either to the preceding or to the following verb. This means that *so far as the Greek words are concerned* they can be punctuated either way. Therefore the error of the KJV punctuation is not the result of mistranslating the Greek *words* but rather a failure to appreciate that Jesus was speaking Aramaic and using a familiar Old Testament idiom.[1]

The translators of the Old Testament however had no difficulty in recognizing this idiom. Thus, in the English translations of Deut. 4:26 and Deut. 8:19, quoted above, they inserted the word, 'that', in order to give the correct sense of the idiom.

In addition to introducing a contradiction, the common mis-translation of the promise to the thief seriously distorts Bible truth concerning the nature of death and the after-life.

Having ascertained the correct translation we are now in a position to examine the passage in detail and determine exactly what Jesus promised the thief. To do this we shall seek answers to three questions:

1. What was the thief's request?

2. What did Jesus mean by paradise?

3. Where did Jesus go on the day of his death?

Answers to these questions will necessitate a close look at the meanings of the New Testament words which are translated 'kingdom', 'paradise', 'hell' and 'soul'.

---

1. The emphatic 'today' is only one of many Hebrew idioms ('hebraisms') found in the New Testament. Jesus and his disciples were Jews steeped in the Old Testament and their language is rich in Hebrew idiom. For example, we have the expression 'son of', 'children of', or 'daughter of' to indicate the character of a person. In both the Old Testament and New Testament we read about 'children of Belial' meaning worthless people. Jesus called those who gave hospitality to missionaries 'sons of peace' (Luke 10:6), and he named James and John Zebedee 'sons of thunder' (Mark 3:17) - an appropriate name for these two disciples who called on Jesus to consume the Samaritans by bringing down fire from heaven (Luke 9:54).

1. What was the thief's request?

This is very important because it is the basis of our Lord's answer. The thief said to Jesus, "Lord, remember me *when you come into your kingdom.*" Although the kingdom that Jesus proclaimed began with lives transformed by his teaching (see Matt. 13:44-46 and Luke 16:16), the coming of Jesus in his kingly power is clearly a future event occurring at his return to the earth when the world will be cleansed from evil (Matt. 13:41-43).

At the Last Supper Jesus said, "I will not drink of the fruit of the vine *until* the kingdom of God comes" (Luke 22:18). His disciples clearly understood the future aspect of his kingdom when they asked Jesus after his resurrection, "Lord, is this the time when you will restore the kingdom to Israel?" (Acts 1:6). Paul likewise viewed the kingdom of Christ as a future event when he wrote to Timothy, "I charge you therefore before God and the Lord Jesus Christ, who will judge the living and the dead, at his appearing and his kingdom ..." (2 Tim. 4:1).

By declaring that Jesus was innocent, the thief showed that he knew Jesus. His request to be rewarded when Christ came into his kingdom implied that he must have heard Jesus preaching and understood the vitally important future aspect of his kingdom.

It needs little imagination to picture this man standing on the fringe of the crowds listening to Jesus preaching the gospel (good news) of the kingdom of God. Perhaps he had been among the multitudes that Jesus had miraculously fed with bread and fish. Perhaps he had been one of those many disciples who took offence at the teaching of Jesus and "turned back and no longer went about with him" (John 6:66). But whoever he was, his request demonstrated a knowledge of Jesus and his teaching. *He did not ask to be taken to heaven, because the gospel he had heard Jesus preach was not about going to heaven but about a transformed earth.*

The thief's petition was granted. He asked to be remembered at the coming of Jesus into his kingdom and this is exactly what Jesus promised him, as will be evident from a study of the word, 'paradise'.

2. What did Jesus mean by Paradise?

As in the case of the word 'kingdom', the meaning of 'paradise' can only be determined by an examination of other Scriptures where the word is used.

The word in Greek is *paradeisos* which is derived from a Persian word meaning 'garden'. The same word is used in the Greek translation of the Old Testament (the Septuagint) in Gen. 2:8 where we read: "And the LORD God planted a garden (*paradeison*) in Eden in the east."

If we consider the changes which will occur at the return of the Lord Jesus Christ we shall see how appropriate was Jesus' description of his kingdom as a paradise or garden. For example, in Revelation we read that at the time the kingdoms of this world are taken over by the Lord Jesus Christ there will be a judgement and rewards and also a time for "destroying those who destroy the earth" (Rev. 11:18). When this happens the earth will be transformed, and will become a new Eden. Hence the promise of our Lord in Rev. 2:7: "To everyone who conquers, I will give permission to eat from the tree of life that is in the paradise of God." The earth restored to Edenic paradise is the ultimate fulfilment of many of the visions of the Old Testament prophets, such as in Isa. 51:3:

> **For the LORD will comfort Zion,**
> **He will comfort all her waste places;**
> **He will make her wilderness like Eden,**
> **And her desert like the garden of the LORD;**
> **Joy and gladness will be found in it,**
> **Thanksgiving and the voice of melody."**

So the promise of Jesus that the thief would be with him in paradise was an appropriate answer to his petition because paradise is such an apt name for the future kingdom of Christ on earth.

There is an interesting reference to paradise in 2 Cor. 12:1-4 where Paul writes:

> ... **I will go on to visions and revelations of the Lord. I know a person in Christ who fourteen years ago was caught up to the third heaven - whether in the body or out of the body I do not know; God knows. And I know that such a person - whether in the body or out of the body I do not know; God knows - was caught up into Paradise and heard things that are not to be told, and that no mortal is permitted to repeat. NRSV**

Here Paul is writing about himself and referring to the fact that he had been given a vision of the future paradise-kingdom of Jesus Christ. He calls this the 'third heaven' because he is using the same metaphor as Peter in 2 Pet. 3 where 'heavens' denote eras of human history. The first heavens represented the world before the flood (v. 5) and the second heavens the Jewish era which was soon to be 'dissolved' (v. 7-12). This will be replaced by the third heavens or paradise when the earth will be restored and there will be "new heavens and a new earth in which righteousness dwells" (v. 13). For a fuller discussion of 'heaven(s)' see Ch. 20.

This brief survey of the meaning of paradise indicates that it has nothing to do with heaven, where God dwells in light unapproachable (1 Tim. 6:16). God's dwelling place is mentioned many times in the Bible but it is never said to be the present or future abode of the righteous. David declared in Psa. 115:16, "The heavens are the LORD's heavens, but the earth he has given to human beings." Peter in Acts 2:34 says. "... David did not ascend into the heavens." Jesus said, "*No one* has ascended into heaven except the one who descended from heaven, the Son of man" (John 3:13).[1]

Matthew refers to the kingdom *of* heaven - not the kingdom *in* heaven. The kingdom of heaven in Matthew is the same as the kingdom of God in Luke (compare Matt. 8:11 with Luke 13:28). Matthew's kingdom of heaven is a heavenly kingdom on earth. In Matt. 5:5 Jesus said, "Blessed are the meek, for they will inherit the earth." And in the same discourse he said, "Rejoice and be glad, for your reward is great in heaven" (verse 12). There is no contradiction here if we follow the rule of comparing Scripture with Scripture, because in Rev. 22:12 Jesus said, "See, I am coming soon; my reward is with me, to repay according to everyone's work." This makes it clear that our reward will be bestowed by Jesus *when he returns to the earth.*

This concept of the reward being reserved or laid up in heaven is also found in the writings of Paul and Peter. Paul in 2 Tim. 4:8 writes:

> **From now on there is reserved for me the crown of righteousness, which the Lord, the righteous judge, will give me on that day, and not only to me but also to all who have longed for his appearing. NRSV**

In 1 Pet. 1:4, Peter describes our hope as "an inheritance that is imperishable, undefiled, and unfading, kept in heaven for you". And in verse 13 he tells us that this reward will be given at the revelation (appearing) of Jesus Christ.

---

1. The descent of Jesus from heaven is explained by verse 34 in the same chapter: "For he whom God has sent speaks the word of God, for God does not give the Spirit by measure." Jesus came from heaven through the descent of the Holy Spirit on Mary, so her child was the Holy One, the Son of God (Luke 1:35).

3. **Where did Jesus go on the day that he died?**

To answer this question we must first study Scripture teaching about the nature of man.

> **And the LORD God formed man of the dust of the ground, and breathed into his nostrils the breath of life; and man became a living soul. Gen. 2:7**

A living soul is not an immortal soul. When man sinned he reverted to dust.

> **In the sweat of your face you shall eat bread Till you return to the ground, For out of it you were taken; For dust you are, And to dust you shall return. Gen. 3:19**

There is no indication that man possesses an immortal soul. The word for deathlessness *athanasia*, occurs only three times in the Bible. In 1 Tim. 6:16 we are told that God alone has immortality *(athanasia)* and from the other two occurrences in 1 Cor. 15:51-54 it is clear that immortality is to be given by God only after the resurrection from the dead.

> **For the trumpet will sound, and the dead will be raised incorruptible, and we shall be changed. For this corruptible must put on incorruption, and this mortal must put on immortality. So when this corruptible has put on incorruption, and this mortal has put on immortality, then shall be brought to pass the saying that is written:** *"Death is swallowed up in victory."*

That the soul of man is not immortal is evident from the words of Jesus in Matt. 10:28: "**Do not fear those who kill the body but cannot kill the soul; but rather fear him who can destroy both soul and body in hell (Gehenna)**". Our souls can suffer the same destruction as our bodies.

This teaching on the nature of man is reinforced by many passages which show that death is the cessation of the life of the whole man - body and mind. For example, in Psa. 146:3,4 we read:

> Put not your trust in princes, nor in the son of man, in whom there is no help. His breath goeth forth, he returneth to his earth; in that very day his thoughts perish. KJV

And Rom. 2:7 makes it clear that immortality is a future hope — not a present possession:

> ... eternal life to those who by patient continuance in doing good seek for glory, honour and immortality.

We can sum up the truth about the myth of the immortal soul by quoting from the Church of England report entitled, *Towards the Conversion of England*, published in 1945. It reads, "**The idea of the inherent indestructibility of the human soul (or consciousness) owes its origin to Greek not to Bible sources.**"

The writer to the Hebrews makes it clear that Jesus, the only begotten Son of God, shared our human nature in every respect:

> Since, therefore, the children share flesh and blood, he himself likewise shared the same things, so that through death he might destroy the one who has the power of death, that is, the devil ... Therefore he had to become like his brothers and sisters in every respect, so that he might be a merciful and faithful high priest in the service of God, to make a sacrifice of atonement for the sins of the people. Heb. 2:14,17 NRSV

His humanity meant that his experience of death would be the same as that of the rest of mankind.

With these facts in mind we can seek an answer to the question of where Jesus went on the day of his death, and look again at the answer Jesus gave in Matt. 12:40:

> **For just as Jonah was three days and three nights in the belly of the sea monster, so for** *three days and three nights the Son of Man will be in the heart of the earth.*
> **NRSV**

Nothing could be clearer than this statement. Jesus did *not* say that his body would be in the heart of the earth and his soul elsewhere; he said the *Son of Man* would be there. 'Son of Man' was a phrase used by Jesus to describe himself (See Matt. 9:6 and 16:27).

This agrees with what Peter said in Acts 2:27 when he applied the words of Psalm 16 to the Lord Jesus: "For you will not abandon my soul to Hades, or let your Holy One experience corruption." In this verse the Greek word *hades* relates to the underworld which became a metaphor for the grave (see Ch.19). The body of Jesus was hidden in the rock tomb of Joseph of Arimathea which was sealed with a large stone. But it was not abandoned; after three days the stone was rolled away and the women who visited the tomb were told, "He is not here, but is risen." (Luke 24:6)

In the Old Testament there is a similar Hebrew word, *Sheol*, which means pit or grave. So it is most appropriate that Jonah, whose incarceration in the belly of the whale was symbolic of Christ's burial, should say, "I called to the LORD out of my distress, and he answered me; out of the belly of Sheol I cried, and you heard my voice."

There are therefore good Scriptural reasons for believing that Jesus meant exactly what he said when he declared that the sign of his authentic Messiahship was the sign of the prophet Jonah and that "as Jonah was three days and three nights in the belly of the sea monster, so for three days and three nights *the Son of Man will be in the heart of the earth.*"

This study of the famous words of Jesus to the thief on the cross reveals that there is no basis for the popular teaching that Jesus promised heaven at death to the penitent thief. This idea originates in a failure to understand the idiomatic use of 'today' in the Bible, and it illustrates the supreme importance of discovering the meaning of Bible words and phrases by comparing Scripture with Scripture and thereby allowing the Bible to interpret itself.

Spirits in prison

On the basis of a passage in the first Epistle of Peter it is widely believed that at his death Jesus descended into hell (*hades*) where he preached to imprisoned souls from the days of Noah — the so-called 'descensus ad inferos'.

> **For Christ also suffered for sins once for all, the righteous for the unrighteous, in order to bring you to God. He was put to death in the flesh, but made alive in the spirit, in which also he went and made a proclamation to the spirits in prison, who in former times did not obey, when God waited patiently in the days of Noah, during the building of the ark, in which a few, that is, eight persons, were saved through water.**
> **1 Pet. 3:18-20 NRSV**

How are we to understand this obscure passage? As with all difficult passages we must seek the meaning of the words and how they are used in other parts of Scripture.

What is meant by *spirit* and *spirits in prison*? Spirit is the Greek word *pneuma* which means 'wind' (John 3:8) but it has many extended meanings in Scripture: for example, breath (2 Thes. 2:8), power of God (Rom. 8:11-13), mind (Mark 8:12), character (Matt. 5:3), angels (Heb. 1:14), 'demon' (Matt. 8:16), life (Luke 8:55). *Pneuma* has many other shades of meaning, but apart from Luke 24:37 (where it refers to a non-existent ghost), **it never refers to disembodied human beings living elsewhere.** When applied to humans it relates to the mind and usually refers to the personality or spiritual character. For example, in 1 John 4:1 John tells his readers to "test the spirits whether they are of God". John is advising them to test the characters of *living people* in their midst.

Who are 'the spirits in prison' to whom Peter refers? They are men and women who are in bondage to sin. They are the spiritually imprisoned who are being offered salvation, as expressed by Isaiah the prophet:

> **I am the LORD, I have called you in righteousness, I have taken you by the hand and kept you; I have given you as a covenant to the people, a light ot the nations, to open the eyes that are blind, to bring out the prisoners from the dungeon, from the prison those who sit in darkness. Isa. 42:6,7 NRSV**

So we ask — how did the spiritually destitute people living before the Flood receive the message of salvation? A clue will be found in the first chapter of the same letter where Peter writes,

> **The prophets who prophesied of the grace that was to be yours searched and enquired about this salvation; they enquired what person or time was indicated by the *Spirit of Christ within them* when predicting the sufferings of Christ and the subsequent glory.**
> **1 Pet. 1:10,11 RSV**

The message of hope for those living before the Flood was given by God's prophets who were imbued with the spirit of Christ. As Peter explains in the same passage in 1 Pet. 3:21, the offer of salvation from the waters of the Flood was a figure of Christ's offer of salvation through the waters of baptism.

Who then were the prophets before the flood who preached in the Spirit of Christ? Noah was clearly one of these and he is described by Peter in his second epistle as a 'preacher of righteousness' (2 Pet. 2:5). But it is significant that in a parallel chapter in Jude we are told that Enoch (the grandfather of Noah) was also a preacher who issued warnings of impending judgement on ungodly sinners who lived before the flood:

> It was of these also that Enoch in the seventh generation from Adam prophesied, saying, "Behold, the Lord came with his holy myriads, to execute judgement on all, and to convict all the ungodly of all their deeds of ungodliness which they have committed in such an ungodly way, and of all the harsh things which ungodly sinners have spoken against him."
> Jude 14,15 RSV.

Homoeoteluton error?

That Enoch might have been the prophet to whom Peter was referring in 1 Pet. 3:19 is supported by an interesting theory of Dr. Rendel Harris. He suggested that Peter originally wrote, "In which also *Enoch* went and preached to the spirits in prison ...".

'In which also' in the original uncial Greek was written ENWKAI. This is similar to the name Enoch which was ENWX. So 'in which also Enoch' would originally have been written thus, ENWKAIENWX.

It is easy to imagine that in copying this sentence a scribe might have failed to write the name "Enoch" thinking he had already written it. This error of omitting repeated similar words or phrases is a well recognized copyists' failing. It is called a homoeoteleuton error.[1] A typical homoeoteleuton error occurs in the 1525 edition of Tyndale's New

---

1. *Homoeoteleuton* is from a combination of the Greek words *homoios* (meaning "like") and *teleutē* (meaning "ending"), i.e. words with similar endings.

Testament where John 14:2,3 should read, "I go to prepare a place for you. And if I go and prepare a place for you, I will come again and receive you unto myself." Whereas Tyndale wrote, "I go to prepare a place for you. I will come again, and receive you unto myself ...". A more recent example appeared in the first printing of the 1988 *New Welsh Bible* where, in Ezek. 5:2, one of the three repeated phrases was omitted.

Whether Peter was referring to Noah or Enoch does not really matter. What we should understand is that this passage need not be interpreted as teaching that Jesus, at his death, went to preach to the disembodied spirits of men and women living before the Flood. This fantastic idea not only introduces a serious contradiction of Matt. 12:40, but is also illogical; why would Jesus preach only to those who had lived before the Flood?

CHAPTER 17

METAPHOR

Metaphor is a figure of speech where words are applied to different spheres. It comes from the Greek, meaning to 'transfer or change'. Metaphor is the commonest figure of speech and is easily recognizable in such expressions as 'stone dead', 'germ of an idea', 'over the top', 'broken heart' and so forth.

Metaphors are effective because they provide emphasis by drawing parallels. They are often decorative and as such are frequent components of poetry as, for example, in Alfred Noyes's *The Highwayman*, which begins:

> The wind was a torrent of darkness among the gusty trees,
> The moon was a ghostly galleon tossed upon cloudy seas,
> The road was a ribbon of moonlight over the purple moor,
> And the highwayman came riding —
> Riding — riding —
> The highwayman came riding up to the old inn door.

The O.T. poetical books are full of metaphor. Psa. 23 is a good example; it includes ten words used metaphorically. Words such as shepherd, green pastures, still waters, rod and staff, etc. are used to build up a picture of divine protection. Metaphors are word pictures in which concrete words are used to illustrate abstract ideas. Although the Hebrew language has few abstract terms it does not suffer as a result. In both prose and poetry it makes excellent use of metaphors for the effective expression of abstract ideas. Consider, for example, the powerful thrust of Rehoboam's threat to those who asked him to ease their burdens. "My little finger shall be thicker than my father's loins ... my father chastised you with whips, but I will chastise you with scorpions." 1 Kin. 12:10,11

Many Bible metaphors are taken from the human body. Thus 'heart' = inner man, i.e. hidden man or true man (e.g. Matt. 15:19), 'bowels' = emotions or feelings — especially affection (Col. 3:12), 'stiffnecked' = stubborn (Exod. 32:9), 'kidneys' (reins) = mind (Psa. 16:7), 'dead' = lost

(Luke 9:60 and 15:24) and the 'body of Christ' = the followers of Christ (Eph. 5:30).

Other metaphors are taken from natural phenomena, for example, 'sea and waves' = people or nations (Isa. 60:5 and Luke 21:25), 'covered by the sea' = conquered (Jer. 51:42), 'mountains and hills' = nation of Israel (Isa. 55:12), 'eagle's wings' = divine protection (Exod. 19:4), 'fountains of living waters' = source of eternal life (Jer. 2:13) and 'rock of thy strength' = divine support (Isa. 17:10). In Ezek. 36:8 we find an interesting example of a 'mixed metaphor',

> **But ye, O mountains of Israel, ye shall shoot forth your branches, and yield your fruit to my people of Israel. KJV**

The Metaphors of John's Gospel

Jesus was particularly fond of using metaphors. In John 10 he spoke of himself as the 'good shepherd' and his followers as 'sheep', and then extended the metaphor to include the 'door of the sheepfold' (also himself), the 'sheepfold' (the church), 'robbers' (persecutors of the church) and 'hireling shepherds' (false teachers).

In another extended metaphor he described himself as 'the vine' (John 15:1) and in yet another he described himself as the 'bread of life which came down form heaven' (John 6:35).

As we showed in Ch.1 the metaphors of John's Gospel were frequently misunderstood by those who heard Jesus speaking. This applied to opponents who deliberately distorted his words as when Jesus said, "Destroy this temple, and in three days I will raise it up" (John 2:19) and later accused him of blaspheming against the temple (Matt. 26:61). It also applied to sympathetic hearers, such as the woman at the well (John 4:15), to Nicodemus (John 3:4) and also to his intimate disciples (John 11:12). It is therefore not surprising that the metaphors of John's Gospel continue to be a source of misunderstanding today.

Metaphors need to be interpreted. When Jesus said, "Very truly, I tell you, unless you eat the flesh of the Son of Man and drink his blood, you have no life in you" (John 6:53), he was using Biblical metaphors. 'Flesh' represents the body or person and 'blood' represents the life which animates it. So eating the flesh of Jesus symbolizes our unity with Jesus who was the word made flesh. Drinking his blood symbolizes our receiving the gift of life through the shedding of his blood.

By taking these metaphors literally the Roman Church formulated the doctrine of transubstantiation which teaches that when the priest consecrates the bread and wine they are miraculously transformed into the flesh and blood of Christ. And we are told that they deny the cup to the laity on the grounds that the blood of Christ might be spilt, with dire consequences.

The Sleep of Death

Because metaphors draw parallels between different things we must not assume that the things that are compared are parallel in all respects. For example, when Jesus said, "Our friend Lazarus has fallen asleep ..." he is using sleep as a metaphor for death. The parallel concepts are that in both death and sleep the subject is unconscious and has no knowledge of existence or time. However, although a sleeper is still alive and breathing, it would be quite wrong to argue that a dead person is still alive, albeit in another sphere. We know from other Scriptures that, apart from a future resurrection, death is the end of life, breathing ceases and thoughts cease:

> **Put not your trust in princes, nor in the son of man, in whom there is no help. His breath goeth forth, he returneth to his earth; in that very day his thoughts perish. Psa. 146:3-4 KJV**

So although death and resurrection are likened to sleep and waking from sleep (Dan. 12:2) there is clearly no exact parallel between sleep and death (see Chs. 16 and 19 for Bible teaching on the death state).

CHAPTER 18

FLESH

'Flesh' is a common Bible metaphor which has several shades of meaning. The literal meaning of flesh (Gk. *sarx*) is the soft tissue of the body as distinct from bone and blood — as in Luke 24:39,

> **Behold, my hands and my feet that it is I myself. Handle me and see, for a spirit does not have flesh and bones as you see me have.**

In the N.T. 'flesh' is almost always used metaphorically, with many subtle differences in emphasis.

1. Flesh may simply be extended to mean animal bodies, as in 1 Cor. 15:39,

   > **All flesh is not the same flesh, but there is one kind of flesh of men, another flesh of beasts, another of fish, and another of birds. KJV**

2. More specifically, flesh is used as a metaphor for the human body, as in John 1:14, "And the Word became flesh and dwelt among us, and we beheld his glory ...".

3. It may refer to the human race in general, as in Luke 3:6, "And all flesh shall see the salvation of God."

4. More commonly, the metaphor is extended into the moral sphere and refers to man's animal, as opposed to his spiritual, nature as in Rom. 8:1,

   > **There is therefore no condemnation to those who are in Christ Jesus, who do not walk according to the flesh, but according to the Spirit.**

So in the N.T. 'flesh' usually stands for those aspects of our nature which derive from our animal instincts and which are manifested by self-gratification in all its forms. Flesh is therefore often linked with sin, as when Paul refers to 'sin in the flesh' and 'sinful flesh' (Rom. 8:3) and both Peter and Paul refer to the 'filthiness of the flesh' (1 Pet. 3:21, 2 Cor. 7:1).

Although flesh is used as a metaphor for sin-tending human nature it would be a mistake to argue that literal flesh is necessarily unclean of itself.[1] Our literal flesh is no different from the flesh of animals. It is the mind that controls the body; our sinful desires come from our 'fleshly *minds*' (Col. 2:18). So theological arguments as to whether human flesh is 'clean' or 'unclean' are meaningless because literal flesh is neutral; it is neither clean nor unclean. Nor is there any scriptural evidence for the theory that Jesus' human flesh was unique in being 'clean'. (See Ch.8.)

However, when the Bible uses 'flesh' as a metaphor for human nature then 'flesh' is certainly not clean. Like Adam we have the inborn impulses to follow our own selfish instincts rather than God's commandments. Paul calls this the 'carnal mind' which is 'enmity against God' (Rom. 8:7).

When we read Paul's discourse on the conflict between flesh and spirit in Rom. 7 and 8 it is easy to overlook the fact that he is using flesh as a metaphor for human nature; the conflict is between the fleshly or carnal mind and the spiritual mind. Paul expresses this antithesis most clearly in Rom. 8:5,6:

> **For those who live according to the flesh set their minds on the things of the flesh, but those who live according to the Spirit, the things of the Spirit. For to be carnally minded is death, but to be spiritually minded is life and peace.**

---

1. The reference to 'our vile body' in Phil. 3:21 is explained by the fact that the original meaning of vile was 'of low status or value'. The word in the Greek, *tapeinos*, is used by Mary in Luke 1:48 to describe her low social status (KJV 'low estate').

Because Jesus partook of flesh and blood and was made in all things like his brethren (Heb. 2:14,17) he shared our human nature and was tempted as we are (Heb. 2:18) and it was by the complete conquest of these impulses to sin that he destroyed the power of sin which assailed him. This victory over sin is described in Heb. 2:14:

> **Inasmuch then as the children have partaken of flesh and blood, he himself likewise shared the same, that through death he might destroy him who has the power of death, that is the devil.**

Jesus destroyed the devil by totally conquering the impulses to sin which were part of his human nature. He was the only one who could completely conquer these impulses, but in following Jesus we must also strive to destroy the devil within each of us.[1]

> **For if you live according to the flesh you will die; but if by the Spirit you put to death the deeds of the body, you will live. Rom. 8:13**

What is 'sin'?

Sin is the transgression of God's law. As we have seen (ch. 3) the animals are subject only to implanted instincts over which they have no control, but God has given man laws which are designed to raise us above the animals by giving us control over our instincts and the ability to distinguish right from wrong and make moral choices. If we live solely as the animals and only follow our natural selfish instincts then we have 'carnal minds'. There is clearly no virtue in such lives, as the Psalmist declared,

> **Man that is in honour and understandeth not, is like the beasts that perish. Psa. 49:20 KJV**

---

1. For a fuller exposition of the devil and Satan see Chapter 29.

Paul's use of 'flesh' as a metaphor for the carnal mind is evident in Gal. 5:19-21 where he provides a list of the 'works of the flesh',[1]

> **Now the works of the flesh are evident, which are: adultery, fornication, uncleanness, licentiousness, idolatry, sorcery, hatred, contentions, jealousies, outbursts of wrath, selfish ambitions, dissensions, heresies, envy, murders, drunkenness, revels, and the like ...**

Sadly our ability to control our instincts carries with it the capacity to abuse them, so we see that most of these vices are not just uncontrolled animal instincts but are *perverted* instincts which make them far worse than anything found in the animal kingdom. It should also be noted that only three, possibly four, of these seventeen vices are sexual offences. It is therefore regrettable that Christians have tended to put such a disproportionate emphasis on sexual offences with the imposition of severe punishments for sexual offenders and giving special status to celibacy. This preoccupation with sex reached its most extreme form with the American 'Shakers' of the 18th. and 19th. centuries who advocated celibacy for all their members.

'Original Sin'

A misunderstanding of the metaphorical use of 'flesh' has led to several errors such as the Augustinian doctrine of 'original sin' which taught that the fall in Eden contaminated human flesh. This led to the practice of asceticism which was designed to 'punish' the body.

---

1. It is interesting to note that when our Lord gave a similar list of human vices, in Mark 7:21-23, he used a different metaphor; he described them as coming 'from within, out of the *heart* of man'. There is no contradiction between Jesus and Paul; both metaphors refer to the propensity for evil which resides in the minds of us all.

Augustine went even further and taught that the Fall changed the physiology of our sex drive by introducing lust or 'shameful appetite'. He wrote that, if there had been no Fall, "the seed of generation should have been sown in the vessel, as corn is now in the field ... Man therefore would have sown the seed, and the woman have received it, as need required, without any lust, and as their wills desired."[1] It is no wonder that such teaching resulted in sexual activity, even within marriage, becoming loaded with guilt feelings.

The doctrine of 'original sin' also gave rise to the Roman Catholic doctrines of the 'Immaculate Conception' and 'Perpetual Virginity'. Immaculate Conception (promulgated ex Cathedra in 1854) teaches that Mary was uncontaminated by sin from the moment of her conception. Perpetual Virginity (adopted by the Council of Chalcedon in 451) teaches that Mary never had sexual relations with Joseph (See Ch.33 for a refutation of this doctrine).

Pelagius, an early 5th century British theologian, was the chief opponent of the Augustinian doctrine that we are all guilty and suffer death because of Adam's sin. But he failed to appreciate that man was created with animal instincts which if not controlled lead to sin. As well as denying inherited *guilt* Pelagius also denied our inherited *nature*. In this way he wrongly concluded that man had a natural capacity to be sinless.

Other reasons for rejecting the doctrine of 'original sin' as propounded by Augustine have been considered in dealing with the Infinitive Absolute idiom (Ch.12).

---

1. *The City of God*, Trans. J Healey, Dent 1972, Vol.2. p.54.

CHAPTER 19

HELL

In the English Bible the word 'hell' is used to translate three different Bible words, namely *Sheol* in the O.T. and *Hades* and *Gehenna* both in the N.T. *Sheol* is a Hebrew word meaning pit or grave, *Hades* is a Greek metaphor for the grave and *Gehenna* is a metaphor for destruction.

Much confusion has arisen because Tyndale and most subsequent English Bibles have failed to distinguish clearly between Sheol and Hades on the one hand and Gehenna on the other. Since there are no equivalent words in the English language it is safer to adopt the practice of the Emphatic Diaglott, Young's Literal Translation and Weymouth versions which leave the words untranslated.

We shall briefly consider these three words translated 'hell'.

Sheol

Sheol is a poetic Hebrew word meaning the grave. It is a place of oblivion, as Hezekiah recognized in his prayer of thanksgiving for fifteen years' extension of life.

> **I said in the cutting off of my days, I shall to to the gates of the grave (Sheol): I am deprived of the residue of my years ... For the grave (Sheol) cannot praise thee, death cannot celebrate thee; they that go down to the pit cannot hope for thy truth. Isa. 38:10,18 KJV**

Sheol is not associated with punishment; both good men (Jacob, Gen. 37:35) and bad men (Korah, Num. 16:30) go there. It is the destiny of all who die. In 31 out of 65 occasions where Sheol is found in the O.T. the KJV translates it by 'grave'. In another 31 cases it is translated 'hell' and in 3 cases 'pit'. But in all cases grave is an appropriate translation of Sheol. On two occasions it is used metaphorically. In Jonah 2:2 Jonah 'cried out of the belly of Sheol' (the whale) and in a poetic passage in Ezek. 32:21 the prophet imagines slain Egyptians crying out of Sheol.

Hades

Hades is the Greek word for the dark and dismal abode of Pluto, the God of the underworld in Greek mythology. Thus Hades became an appropriate biblical metaphor for the grave and like Sheol it is a place of oblivion or unconsciousness.[1] That Hades has the same meaning as Sheol is shown by the Greek Septuagint which used Hades for Sheol. For example in Psa. 6:5 'grave' is *Sheol* in Hebrew and *Hades* in Greek.

> **For in death there is no remembrance of thee; in the grave who shall give thee thanks? KJV**

Both Sheol and Hades have gates. The gates can be opened and the dead raised. David was confident that God would redeem him from the power of Sheol (Psa. 49:15). Hezekiah spoke of the gates of Sheol (Isa. 38:10). As Jonah was not left in the 'belly of Sheol' (Jonah 2:2) so Jesus was not left in Hades (Acts 2:27). Jesus affirmed that the 'gates of Hades' would not prevail against his church (Matt. 16:18). In Rev. 1:18 Jesus assures us that he has the keys to the gates of Hades and death. And in his solemn warning to Capernaum in Matt. 11:23,24 he said the city would be cast down to Hades but would be brought back from there on the day of judgement.

---

1. The only exception to this concept of Hades as the grave is found in Luke 16:23 where Jesus relates a parable in which there is an imaginary conversation in Hades involving a rich man, a beggar named Lazarus and Abraham. This parable is based on Jewish myths. It is heavily ironic and obviously not intended to be understood literally. This is dealt with in Ch.25.

Gehenna (hell fire)

Gehenna is a metaphor which has given rise to serious and tragic misunderstandings. It has commonly been interpreted as a place of never-ending torment for unrepentant sinners. *Gehenna* is the Latin and English transliteration of the Greek *Géenna*, itself a transliteration of the Hebrew *Ge-hinnom* or valley of Hinnom which was a steep valley south of Jerusalem where children had been sacrificed by fire to Moloch (2 Chr. 28:3) and which was made into a refuse tip during the reforms of Josiah (2 Kin. 23:10). Later it became a symbol for the place of torture and suffering for wicked souls — a myth which the Jewish rabbis adopted from their Babylonian and Persian conquerors (see Ch. 30). But Jesus rejected rabbinic tradition. He based all his doctrine on the Old Testament and would never have accepted this pagan mythology.

In Mark 9:43-48 Jesus says,

> **If your hand causes you to stumble, cut it off; it is better for you to enter life maimed than to have two hands and to go to hell (Gehenna), to the unquenchable fire. And if your foot causes you to stumble, cut it off; it is better for you to enter life lame than to have two feet and to be thrown into hell (Gehenna). And if your eye causes you to stumble, tear it out; it is better for you to enter the kingdom of God with one eye than to have two eyes and be thrown into hell (Gehenna) where their worm never dies, and the fire is never quenched.   NRSV**

In this passage Jesus uses a metaphor taken from the last verse of Isaiah who lived long before the Jews adopted the horrific pagan concepts of the underworld:

> **And they shall go forth and look**
> **Upon the corpses of the men**
> **Who have transgressed against me.**
> **For their worm does not die,**
> **And their fire is not quenched.**
> **They shall be an abhorrence to all flesh.   Isa. 66:24**

In this verse Isaiah is consigning *carcases*, not living souls, to everlasting destruction. Like Isaiah, Jesus is talking about destruction. There is no suggestion of torture.

From our own experience of fire it should be evident that fire is an appropriate metaphor for destruction rather than torture. Fire is an agent of destruction because it destroys organic matter and refines metal by destroying impurities (Ezek. 22:18). It would be an utterly inappropriate metaphor for endless torture.[1]

Jesus' use of Gehenna as a metaphor for destruction was particularly appropriate because in his day the bodies of executed criminals were thrown out of the Jerusalem dung gate onto the Gehenna refuse tip. As in all rubbish tips, methane gas would be generated from the fermentation of organic matter so that from time to time bursts of flame would emerge from the smouldering tip. This would have been a familiar sight to his listeners.

We note that Jesus also refers to the presence of worms in Gehenna. Worms would not be found nor would they survive in traditional hell fire, but in a rubbish tip worms are part of the biological process of the breakdown of organic matter.

The words, 'where their worm does not die and the fire is not quenched', are often used to teach that hell torments are endless. But surely the endlessness refers to the destruction; Jesus is emphasizing the irreversible nature of the destructive process.

---

1. Augustine, aware of this problem, wrote, "If therefore the salamander live in the fire (as the most exact naturalists record), and if there be certain famous hills in Sicily that have been on fire continually, and yet remain whole and unconsumed, then are these sufficient proof to show that all does not consume that burns, as the soul proves that all that feels pain does not perish." *City of God*, Trans. J Healey, Dent, Vol.2 p.322.

The concept of never-ending torture in hell is a blasphemy against the character of God. It is undeniable that the God of the Bible is just and merciful. Eternal torment is incompatible with both these characteristics. Torture for infinity (a billion years is a speck of infinity) as a punishment for a few years of rebellion against God is clearly unjust; endless torture by fire cannot be the work of a merciful God.

The ghastly concept of never-ending hell torments is thus a figment of the imagination derived from a literal interpretation of metaphors and reinforced by the pagan concept of the devil as a god of evil who presides over a mythical underworld.

It is sometimes argued that total rejection of God merits total punishment. True, but that is exactly what death involves when it is understood as annihilation.

Belief in eternal torment has had two tragic consequences. On the one hand it has caused some to abandon Christianity as a repulsive religion,[1] and on the other hand it has caused so-called Christians to torture and burn those who did not accept their dogmas. The ruthless logical basis for torture by fire, i.e. burning at the stake, is simple. If rejection of Christianity merits never-ending torture by fire in hell then a relatively short period of suffering to achieve conversion is more than justified.

Conclusion

This short study of hell demonstrates the vital importance of distinguishing between the two different metaphors which have so often been conflated by translators. Although both refer to what happens after death they relate to entirely different aspects. Sheol and Hades are metaphors for the grave which will receive all of us and out of which we

---

1. One of the reasons for Darwin's final rejection of Christianity was his belief that the Bible taught hell torments (See *Darwin*, A. Desmond and J. Moore, Penguin 1992, pp 360, 376, 378).

hope to emerge to everlasting life. Gehenna on the other hand is a metaphor for destruction and is the destiny of those who are unrepentant and will suffer 'everlasting contempt' (Dan. 12:2).

The distinction between Hades and Gehenna is clearly seen in Matt. 10:28:

> **And do not fear those who kill the body but cannot kill the soul. But rather fear him who is able to destroy both soul and body in hell (Gehenna).**

We should have no fear of Hades whose gates can be opened, but rather we should fear God who is able to cast us into Gehenna, the lake of fire into which death and hell (Hades) will be cast when "God shall wipe away all tears from their eyes and there shall be no more death, neither sorrow nor crying." Rev. 20:14 and 21:4.

CHAPTER 20

HEAVEN(S) AND EARTH

In both Old and New Testaments the words translated heaven or heavens are used in three different ways:

1. The physical heaven, i.e. the realm above the earth;
2. God's dwelling place;
3. A metaphor for political and religious institutions.

1. The physical heaven was created in the beginning (Gen. 1:1). Heaven contains the sun, moon and stars and is the source of light (Gen. 1:4); it contains cloud and is the source of rain (Deut. 11:11). The literal heaven is often described in metaphorical language as having 'windows' (sluice gates, Gen. 7:11), and 'pillars' (Job 26:11).

2. More specifically heaven refers to God's throne as in Matt. 5:34 and God's dwelling as in Deut. 4:39. Throughout the Bible it is clear that God's abode is inaccessible to man (1 Tim. 6:16) and that no man has ascended into heaven (John 3:13). Heaven is also used by metonymy (Ch.22) as in Matthew who uses 'kingdom of heaven' as equivalent to Luke's 'kingdom of God'.

3. It is when heaven is used as a metaphor that difficulties may occur, as in Hag. 2:6,7

> **For thus saith the LORD of hosts; Yet once, it is a little while, and I will shake the heavens, and the earth, and the sea, and the dry land; And I will shake all nations, and the desire of all nations shall come: and I will fill this house with glory, saith the LORD of hosts. Hag. 2:6,7 KJV**

Haggai is referring to the restoration of Israel after their return from Babylon and the rebuilding of the temple. He was a prophet of the Restoration and his mission was to encourage this rebuilding (Ezra 5:1 and 6:14). In the last of his four proclamations (Hag. 2:20-23) the prophet, using similar words, again encouraged Zerubbabel to complete the building of the temple.

> **Speak to Zerubbabel governor of Judah saying, I will shake the heavens and the earth; And I will overthrow the throne of kingdoms, and I will destroy the strength of the kingdoms of the heathen ... KJV**

The shaking of the heavens and the earth clearly refers to the defeat of the Samaritan opposition to the building of the temple (Ezra 6:15).

The writer of the Epistle to the Hebrews quotes these words and relates them to the end of the Mosaic era and the establishment of 'a kingdom which cannot cannot be shaken' (Heb. 12:25-28). In both cases heaven is used as a metaphor for the political and religious order of the day which was undergoing dramatic change. There will, of course, be a third and even greater shaking of the political and religious heavens at the return of Jesus Christ and the end of Gentile times (Luke 21:24-27).

In Matt. 11:23 Jesus uses 'heaven' as a metaphor for the pride of the unrepentant inhabitants of Capernaum in these words:

> **And you, Capernaum, who are exalted to heaven, will be brought down to Hades ... Matt. 11:23**

The fulfilment of this prophecy can be seen today in the ruins of this once important town.

Another example of the metaphorical use of heaven and earth is found in Joel 2:30:

> **And I will show wonders in the heavens and in the earth, blood and fire and pillars of smoke. KJV**

Peter quotes this verse in Acts 2:19 to show that it applied to the momentous events on the day of Pentecost — events which were a foretaste of the age to come (Heb. 6:5).

In Isa. 51:6 the prophet describes the end of human government in terms of the heavens vanishing away like smoke and the earth growing old like a garment, and in Isa. 65:17 he describes the Messianic Age as follows:

> **For behold, I create new heavens and a new earth; And the former shall not be remembered or come to mind.**

In spite of many examples in Scripture of heavens and earth being used as metaphors for political and religious dispensations, the figure is not always recognized. Heb. 1:10-12 contains an important example of this metaphor which has been taken literally:

> **And, Thou, Lord, in the beginning hast laid the foundation of the earth; and the heavens are the works of thine hands: They shall perish; but thou remainest; and they all shall wax old as doth a garment; And as a vesture thou shalt fold them up, and they shall be changed: but thou art the same, and thy years shall not fail. KJV**

To understand these verses we need to bear in mind that the theme of the letter to the Hebrews is — *Christ fulfils the law of Moses*. Hebrews deals with the end of the law of Moses — not with the end of the material world. So the 'heavens and earth' which are to perish represent the Mosaic religious order. This is confirmed by the writer's use of the same metaphor in 12:25-26 where there is no doubt that he is referring to the end of the Mosaic dispensation and the establishment of the Kingdom of Christ which "cannot be shaken" (v. 27).

> See that ye refuse not him that speaketh. For if they escaped not who refused him that spake on earth (at Sinai v. 18), much more shall not we escape if we turn away from him that speaketh from heaven: whose voice then shook the earth: but now he hath promised saying, YET ONCE MORE I SHAKE NOT THE EARTH ONLY, BUT ALSO HEAVEN. KJV

Heb. 1:10-12 is a quotation from Psa. 102:25-27 which refers to God's original creation. The Psalmist is using poetic hyperbole (ch. 27) to contrast the everlasting God with His perishable creation. The writer to the Hebrews gives this passage a Messianic meaning appropriate to his theme. He contrasts the eternal rule of the Son of God with the temporary Mosaic dispensation which was about to be folded up as a garment.

One might ask how we should understand that Jesus laid the foundations of the Mosaic heavens and earth? The answer is simple. Most of the Epistle to the Hebrews is an exposition of the fact that Jesus Christ was the substance of which the Mosaic dispensation was but a shadow. The tabernacle and its furniture and the sacrifices and the high priest were merely 'a shadow of good things to come' (Heb. 10:1). All pointed forwards to Jesus Christ.

There is no compelling evidence that Psa. 102 and Heb. 1 support the theory that God has planned to destroy the earth. And there is no evidence in the rest of Scripture that the literal heavens and earth will perish. On the contrary God has sworn on no less than three occasions, "As truly as I live, all the earth shall be filled with the glory of the LORD" (Num. 14:21, Hab. 2:14, Isa. 11:9). There is therefore no justification for arguing that Heb. 1:10-12 teaches that Jesus Christ was the Creator of the literal heavens and earth which he would later destroy.

Another misinterpretation of heavens and earth, in 2 Pet. 3:7-12, has led to the unwarranted assumption that the earth will be destroyed by fire. Peter warns his contemporaries of imminent disaster:

> But the heavens and the earth which are now preserved by the same word, are reserved for fire until the day of judgement and perdition of ungodly men. But, beloved, do not forget this one thing, that with the Lord one day is as a thousand years, and a thousand years as one day.

In this chapter Peter is dealing with the coming judgements of the Lord and the overthrow of the Jewish state. And in this connection he is drawing a parallel between the destruction of human society in the days of Noah, when the world (Gk. *kosmos* = social order) was destroyed by water, and the coming destruction in AD 70 when the Jewish heavens "will pass away with a great noise, and the elements will melt with fervent heat; both the earth and the ones that are in it will be burned up" (v. 10).

This prophecy was dramatically fulfilled by the Roman General, Titus when he brought about the holocaust that destroyed Jerusalem in AD 70. Anyone who doubts the appropriateness of the metaphors of 2 Pet. 3:10-12 to the destruction of Jerusalem and the temple in AD 70 should read Josephus's account in *Wars of the Jews*, Book 6, Ch. 5.

The destruction of the Jewish state in AD 70 was predicted by Jesus by parable (Luke 20:16) and by direct prophecy (Matt. 24 and Luke 21). It would be difficult to exaggerate the catastrophic nature of this event for the Jewish people. Their temple was destroyed, over a million Jews were killed, 100,000 were sold into slavery and the remainder were expelled from their country. Intimations and warnings of this disaster are found throughout the N.T. In Matt. 24:3 and 1 Cor. 10:11 it is called *'the end of the world'* (Gk. *aiōn* = age), John calls it *'the last time'* (1 John 2:18) and Peter warns his readers that *"the end of all things is at hand"* (1 Pet. 4:7).

The immediacy and urgency of Peter's words in 2 Pet. 3 indicate that the 'last days' of which he was speaking related to events which were shortly to happen. However, there is no doubt that, as in the Olivet prophecy in

Luke 21, the events of the last days of Judah's kingdom will find their parallel in the last days of Gentile times in which we live. It is significant that in this chapter Peter refers to three different 'heavens and earth' which relate to different periods of Bible history. Verses 5-6 refer to the antediluvian era, vv. 7-12 relate to the Mosaic dispensation and v. 14 takes us forward into the millenium. As suggested in Ch. 16 it is likely that Paul's reference in 2 Cor. 12:1-4 to his being caught up into a paradisical 'third heaven' refers to a vision of the millenium similar to the vision of the Kingdom given to Peter, James and John at the transfiguration (Matt. 16:28).

The lesson of 2 Pet. 3 is for all time. As each era draws to its close God issues warnings of impending judgement which are ignored. Noah, a 'preacher of righteousness' was spurned by an ungodly world full of violence (2 Pet. 2:5 and Gen. 6:11). Jesus wept over Jerusalem but his efforts to save his people culminated in his crucifixion. And now at the end of Gentile times our own violent society is wilfully ignorant of the Word of God and of judgement to come.

Regrettably the metaphorical language of 2 Pet. 3:10-12 has also been interpreted to mean that the world will be destroyed by fire — possibly a nuclear holocaust. But as we have shown (p.76) the plain language of the Bible predicts a different future. Paul affirms in 1 Cor. 15:24-28 that Christ will reign until he has put all enemies under his feet, and all things are made subject to him. Why would God destroy the earth after it had been cleansed from sin and death?

CHAPTER 21

DIVINE ANTHROPOMORPHISM AND CONDESCENSION

Divine anthropomorphism is a particular kind of metaphor in which human parts, actions and feelings are attributed to God. Thus God is described as having a 'face' (Psa. 10:11), 'eyes' and 'ears' (Ezek. 8:18). God is said to 'hiss' (Isa. 5:26), to 'laugh' (Psa. 2:4) and to 'cry out' (Isa. 42:13). God is also said to be 'zealous' (Isa. 9:7), 'jealous' (Exod. 20:5), 'comforted' (Ezek. 5:13) and 'refreshed' (Exod. 31:17).

These are only a few of very many examples of where God is described in human terms. Generally there is no difficulty in understanding what is meant by these metaphors although we might puzzle as to exactly how we should understand God's 'repentance', as in Gen. 6:6 where we read, 'And it repented the LORD that he made man on the earth, and it grieved him at his heart.'

The reason for these Divine anthropomorphisms is because we humans can have no concept of the true nature of God. His thoughts are so high above ours (Isa. 55:8,9) and His ways so inscrutable (Rom. 11:33) that God is best described through human imagery. Thus when God cut short the plague inflicted on Israel we are told that "the Lord commanded the angel and he put up his sword again into the sheath thereof" (1 Chr. 21:27).

Another name for Divine anthropomorphism is the Greek noun *syncatabasis* which means 'going down together with' hence the Latin name *condescensio* or condescension. These terms express the idea that God is condescending to man's limited mental horizons, as for example in Gen 2:7 when God describes the creation of man:

> **And the LORD God formed man of the dust of the ground, and breathed into his nostrils the breath of life, and man became a living soul.**

Few would argue from this that God created man by gathering dust, producing a body and then giving it life by breathing into it. But the language is very effective in teaching the lesson that our bodies are composed of the elements of the earth, that life is a gift from God and that, when the 'breath of life' is withdrawn, man "returns to his earth; in that very day his thoughts perish." (Psa. 146:4)

God, who "humbles himself to behold the things that are in heaven and in the earth" (Psa. 113:6), provides us with an interesting example of divine condescension in Exod. 19:8,9. Here Moses reports to God the words of the people. Taken literally this suggests that God had not heard the words of the people and that Moses was relaying the information to God.

A very important example of Divine condescension relates to God's use of time. We are time-bound creatures and cannot enter into His timeless dimension. Peter expresses this truth in simple language when he states that "one day is with the LORD as a thousand years, and a thousand years as one day" (2 Pet. 3:8). Statements about God 'remembering' (Gen. 8:1), God's 'patience' (Rom. 15:5) and His 'longsuffering' (Rom. 2:4) are all examples of how God condescends to our time-bound state. These words cannot apply literally to God who knows the end from the beginning. We shall return to this figure of speech when dealing with the days of Genesis 1.

Jewish practices

Christians are not alone in their misunderstanding of Biblical metaphors. In Deut. 6:6-9 we read,

> And these words which I command thee this day, shall be in thine heart ... and thou shalt bind them for a sign upon thine hand, and they shall be as frontlets between thine eyes. And thou shalt write them upon the posts of thy house, and upon thy gates. KJV

Heart, hand, eyes and doorposts are clearly metaphors to teach that the word of God should control all Israel's thoughts and actions. But orthodox Jews have devised elaborate rules for the literal application of these metaphors in the form of *tephilim* and *mezuzoth*. Tephilim are small black leather boxes with four compartments containing Scripture passages on folded parchments. They are worn by the men at prayer every day except Sabbaths. One box is strapped to the mid-forehead just above the hair line and the other is strapped to the non-dominant upper arm two finger breadths above the elbow, with straps extending down to the end of the middle finger. A Mezuza is a small oblong box containing a tiny parchment scroll with Scripture passages.[1] It is fixed to the upper part of the right hand doorpost of every door of the house (except the toilet) and is touched by each person entering the room.

Although this desire to keep God's commandments is sincere, the literal interpretation of the metaphors could have the effect of converting deep spiritual truths into superficial rituals.

Extended metaphor, parable and allegory

An extended metaphor is a combination of metaphors on a theme, as in John 6 (bread, flesh and blood) and John 10 (sheep, shepherd, sheepfold, etc.) The extended metaphors in John's Gospel are called *paroimíais* — translated 'proverbs' in the KJV of John 16:25-29 and 'figures' in the NRSV.

When extended metaphors are used to create stories with hidden meaning they are called *parabolais* (parables). But when a historical event is given a hidden meaning it is called *allegoreo* (allegory). Thus in Scripture a parable is based on a story whereas allegory is based on history.

---

1. The four separate parchments in a tephil contain Exod. 13:1-10, Exod. 13:11-16, Deut. 6:4-9 and Deut. 11:13-20. A mezuza scroll contains Deut. 6:4-9 and Deut. 11:13-21.

The Epistle to the Galatians deals with the problem of Jewish Christians who insisted on keeping the Law of Moses. In Gal. 4:22-31 Paul argued that the history of the two sons of Abraham was an allegory of the conflict between Jews and Christians. Hagar the bondwoman and her son Ishmael represented the Mosaic covenant at Sinai which brought Israel ('Jerusalem which now is') into bondage to sin. Whereas Sarah the freewoman and Isaac her son represented the covenant in Christ whereby we are freed from sin and become children of spiritual Israel ('Jerusalem which is above').

Although this is the only event in Scripture that is called an allegory, it is evident that many other events such as the crossing of the Red Sea (1 Cor. 10:2) and the plague of serpents (John 3:14) contain allegories. And as we have seen, the events described in Gen. 2 and 3 are highly allegorical and provide vital clues to the understanding of sin, death and salvation (Chs. 12 and 13).

CHAPTER 22

METONYMY

Metonymy means change of name and describes a figure of speech which puts one thing for another and in which the substituted word is an object or idea closely connected with that for which it stands. Thus someone who is 'fond of the bottle' is fond of alcohol and the 'bench' stands for magistrates.

Metonymy differs from metaphor only in that there is less change of meaning. When we say that someone is a 'big mouth', meaning boastful, we are using metonymy, whereas when we speak of the 'mouth of a river' we are using metaphor.

There are many examples of metonymy in the Scriptures. In the Old Testament 'sceptre' stands for ruler (Gen. 49:10), and in the New Testament 'circumcision' stands for Jews (Gal. 2:7-9).

Rachel weeping

Jer. 31:15 contains a very interesting metonym:

> **Thus saith the LORD: A voice was heard in Ramah, lamentation and bitter weeping: Rachel weeping for her children refused to be comforted for her children, because they were not. KJV**

In this passage Jeremiah predicted the distress of bereaved Jewish women in Ramah which was to become a transit camp for Jewish prisoners after the destruction of Jerusalem (Jer. 40:1). Ramah is three miles north of Jerusalem in the territory of Benjamin. Since Rachel died giving birth to Benjamin and was buried near Ramah it was appropriate that Rachel, who so longed for children, should have been chosen as a metonym for bereaved Jewish mothers. And it is interesting to note that Matthew tells us that Jeremiah's prophecy had an extended fulfilment in the weeping of the mothers of Bethlehem after Herod's slaughter of their young children (Matt. 2:16-18).

Speaking in tongues

There would seem to be little possibility of misinterpreting metonymy, but the Bible use of the word 'tongues' as a metonym for languages has contributed to a serious misunderstanding.

It is evident from Acts 2 that the Pentecostal 'tongues' were foreign languages given for the express purpose of spreading the gospel among foreigners. Thus in Acts 2:4-6 we read that "they began to speak with other tongues" (Gk. *glōssa)* and as a result "every man heard them speak in his own language" (Gk. *dialektos).*

And yet when Paul discussed this miraculous power of speaking in foreign languages in 1 Cor. 14 many have argued that he was writing about ecstatic utterances in non-existent languages. But a careful reading of this chapter will make it clear that Paul is dealing with abuses of the gift of languages in which converts were speaking foreign languages *within* the church. In other words, they were not using foreign languages to preach to foreigners but to show off among themselves. So Paul states emphatically, "Tongues, then, are a sign not for believers but for unbelievers ..." (1 Cor. 14:22). This verse alone should convince us that the ecstatic (hysterical) utterances of Pentecostals in their meetings have nothing to do with the true purpose of the gift of tongues.

Two factors have contributed to this misunderstanding. The first is the use of the word 'tongues' in Acts 2 and 1 Cor. 14. Although this is a correct literal translation of the Greek *glōssa* we do not normally use this metonymy in English. Thus, we do not say people speak many tongues — we say they speak many languages. The retention of this Biblical idiom in our English translations has probably contributed to the notion that these tongues are not ordinary foreign languages.

The second and more important factor is the use of the expression, 'unknown tongue' in the KJV of 1 Cor. 14. 'Unknown' is not in the original Greek; it is a spurious addition which reinforces the notion that in 1 Cor. 14 Paul is dealing with completely unknown languages.

The fact that the Spirit-guided speaker in a foreign language might not understand what he was saying does not mean that he was speaking an unknown language. It would only be incomprehensible to members of the church, or visitors who did not speak that particular language (1 Cor. 14:23). To a foreigner who spoke the language it would be perfectly comprehensible — as described in Acts 2:11 where they exclaimed, "... in our own languages we hear them speaking about God's deeds of power." (NRSV).

Confusion and ambiguity on this subject is reflected in many translations of the N.T. Thus, the Jerusalem Bible and the Barclay Bible both translate the Greek *'glōssa'* in Acts 2 by the word 'language', but they retain 'tongue' throughout 1 Cor. 14. Phillips also uses the word 'language' in Acts 2 but in 1 Cor. 14 he puts 'tongues' in inverted commas.

Ferrar Fenton alone is consistent in using the words 'language' or 'foreign language' throughout Acts and 1 Cor. 14. It is likely that if all other Bible translators had translated 'tongue' into 'language' then the Pentecostal movement might never have arisen.

CHAPTER 23

IRONY

Irony is a figure of speech in which one gives emphasis by saying something different from what is meant. It comes from the Greek *eirō* = 'I say'; it implies, 'I say one thing but I mean another'. A simple example from everyday speech is, 'You're a fine fellow' meaning the opposite. The true meaning of an ironic statement is conveyed by subtle changes in volume, tempo and tone of voice so that spoken irony is usually easy to recognize. So when the prophet Michaiah said to Ahab, "Go up and triumph; the LORD will give it into the hand of the king", Ahab's reply indicates that he instantly recognized the irony in his voice (1 Kin. 22:15,16).

Similarly, Job's friends would have little difficulty in detecting the bitter irony of Job's exclamation, "No doubt you are the people and wisdom will die with you!" (Job 12:2). Nor would the Israelites have misunderstood the sustained irony in the rebuke of Amos when he said,

> **Come to Bethel — and transgress; to Gilgal — and multiply transgression; bring your sacrifices every morning, your tithes every three days; bring a thank-offering of leavened bread, and proclaim freewill offerings, publish them; for so you love to do, O people of Israel! Amos 4:4,5 NRSV**

A more subtle example of irony is found in Mal. 3:1,

> **Behold, I will send my messenger, and he shall prepare the way before me: and the Lord, whom ye seek, shall suddenly come to his temple, even the messenger of the covenant, whom ye delight in: behold, he shall come, saith the LORD of hosts. KJV**

At his first visit to Jerusalem Nehemiah had rebuilt the walls and sealed a solemn covenant with the Jews who promised to remain faithful (Neh.

9:38 and 10:29). But after Nehemiah's departure they forsook God and broke the covenant. In this passage, Malachi, who was contemporary with Nehemiah is warning these faithless covenant breakers that Nehemiah, the 'messenger of the covenant', would soon return and cleanse the temple which they had polluted. Nehemiah's second visit to Jerusalem is described in Neh. 13:7-31.

The expressions "The Lord whom ye seek" and "the messenger ye delight in" are heavily ironic; far from seeking the LORD and delighting in the covenant, they had abandoned temple worship (Neh. 13:10) and defiled the covenant (Neh. 13:29). So although the cleansing and refining work described in Mal. 3 clearly points forward to the Messiah it had a very real fulfilment in the reforms of Nehemiah at his second visit. Many other examples of irony occur in the O.T., e.g. Lam. 4:21 and Ezek. 28:3.

In the N.T., Paul's epistles to Corinth contain several examples of irony such as in 2 Cor. 11:16-21 where we have sustained and rather bitter irony against false apostles. In 2 Cor. 12:13 there is a gentler irony in his rebuke,

> **How have you been worse off than the other churches, except that I myself did not burden you? Forgive me this wrong!**

Earlier, in 1 Cor. 6:4 Paul rebuked the Corinthians for taking each other to law before worldly judges in these words,

> **If then you have judgements of things pertaining to this life, set them to judge who are least esteemed in the church. KJV**

For the benefit of those who might fail to detect the irony, the NKJV and many other versions except the NIV and Young, change the ironic imperative into a rhetorical question,

> If then you have judgements concerning things pertaining to this life, do you appoint those who are least esteemed by the church to judge?

Although the original Greek allows this translation, the next verse does not support it because Paul continues, "I say this to your shame ...". As Paul was dictating he would realize that his tone of voice would not appear on the written page and so he added this explanation.

An interesting example of irony is found in the words of Pilate in John 19:6. Pilate, frustrated because of his failure to placate the Jews, taunted them with the words,

> **Take him yourselves and crucify him, for I find no crime in him. NRSV**

This was said in spite of the fact that he knew, and they knew, that the Jews had no authority to crucify anyone (John 18:31). We have another use of irony in Matt. 12:27 — see footnote p. 127.

CHAPTER 24

"HERE ARE TWO SWORDS"

In some of Jesus' words at the Last Supper we have an important example of irony which was not only misunderstood by some of those who heard it but has been misunderstood by countless people who have read the words since:

> He said to them, 'But now, the one who has a purse just take it, and likewise a bag. And the one who has no sword must sell his cloak and buy one. For I tell you, this scripture must be fulfilled in me, "And he was counted among the lawless"; and indeed what is written about me is being fulfilled.' They said, 'Lord, look, here are two swords.' He replied, 'It is enough.'
> Luke 22:36-38   NRSV

Here Jesus is apparently telling his followers to buy swords. Such advice would be totally at variance with his teaching as outlined in Matt. 5:38-45. Moreover, when shortly afterwards Peter wielded a sword in his Master's defence, Jesus rebuked him in the strongest terms,

> Put your sword in its place; for all who take the sword will perish by the sword.   Matt. 26:52

Some have argued that in advising them to buy swords Jesus was referring to the changed circumstances after he had left them when their lives would be in danger from persecution. However, the response of Jesus to those who took his life is proof enough that his high moral code of non-violence was not to be abandoned in the face of persecution.

We are therefore drawn to the conclusion that Jesus must have been speaking ironically when he advised his followers to buy swords. Is there evidence from the context or other parts of Scripture to support this idea? A clue is provided by the suggestion of Jesus that they should sell their *garments* to buy swords.

In N.T. times two principal garments were worn. There was the mantle type outer garment, and the inner garment or tunic. These are referred to as 'cloak' (Gk. *himation*) and 'coat' (Gk. *chitōn*) respectively, as in Matt. 5:40, where Jesus says, "And if anyone wants to sue you and take your coat, give your cloak as well." John tells us that at the crucifixion the soldiers rent his outer garment *(himation)* into four parts, but when they found that his tunic *(chitōn)* was woven in one piece they decided to cast lots for it.

We know that the disciples of Jesus had abandoned their occupations and Jesus had commanded them to carry no money or possessions or spare clothing (Luke 9:3), and if they had two coats they were told to share with anyone who had none (Luke 3:11). Therefore in order to buy a sword a disciple of Jesus would have had to sell one of his two garments, and would then be left with only one. It is significant that shortly after the Last Supper two of Jesus' followers were described as possessing only one garment, so it is a reasonable inference that they were the ones who had purchased the two swords.

First there was the 'young man' in Mark 14:51-53 who accompanied Jesus in the Garden of Gethsemane and fled with the other disciples after Jesus was arrested:

> **A certain young man was following him, wearing nothing but a linen cloth. They caught hold of him, but he left the linen cloth and ran off naked. NRSV**

There there was Peter who, after the crucifixion, resumed his occupation as a fisherman, and on hearing that Jesus was on the shore cast himself into the sea:

> **That disciple whom Jesus loved said to Peter, "It is the Lord!" When Simon Peter heard that it was the Lord, he put on some clothes, for he was naked, and jumped into the sea. John 21:7 NRSV**

The fact that Mark alone mentions the incident in the Garden of Gethsemane suggests that he was the young man. And the fact that Mark was a close friend of Peter's (1 Pet. 5:13), and is thought to have obtained details of his Gospel from Peter, supports the suggestion that it was Peter and his young friend Mark who had conspired together to sell their garments and buy swords in order to defend Jesus from arrest.

But why was Peter the leader of this conspiracy? It was because he was absolutely determined that Jesus should not die. He had already affirmed this when, after hearing Jesus describe his impending death at Jerusalem, he said, "Lord, this shall not happen to you." Jesus rebuked Peter with the words, "Get behind me, Satan (adversary)! You are a stumbling block to me; for you are setting your mind not on divine things but on human things." (Matt. 16:22,23 NRSV) And then, just before his arrest, Jesus warned Peter that he would again assume the role of an adversary with the words, "Simon, Simon, behold, Satan hath desired to have you, that he might sift you as wheat." (Luke 22:31). But Peter would not heed the warning. He was determined to go ahead with his plan to rescue Jesus from what he saw as an act of self-destruction. And so with exasperation and irony Jesus turned to the disciples and said, "But now, let him who has a purse take it, and likewise a bag. And let him who has no sword sell his mantle and buy one. For I tell you that this scripture must be fulfilled in me, 'And he was reckoned with transgressors;' for what is written about me has its fulfilment." (Luke 22:36,37 RSV)

So Jesus was telling the conspirators that he knew what they had done and that their determination to use force was a fulfilment of the prophecy that he would be associated with lawless men.[1]

---

1. This is an interesting example of the dual application of an O.T. prophecy. The words, "he was reckoned with transgressors" are taken directly from Isa. 53:12. They obviously refer to the two criminals who were crucified with Jesus. But Jesus showed that they also referred to his closest followers by reason of their plan to use force to resist his arrest.

Peter and Mark would have understood the irony and realized that Jesus was showing that he knew they had sold garments to buy swords, but some of the other disciples may not have known how the swords were obtained and they took Jesus literally, saying, "Lord, look, here are two swords." But Jesus, knowing that Peter was impervious to reason and that nothing would deflect him from his purpose, cut them short with the words, "It is enough", meaning, "Enough of this — there is no point in continuing this conversation."[1] And so, at the moment of arrest, the swords were drawn and Peter struck the first blow in defence of his Master. He missed his target, and a blow that was designed to cleave a skull, only severed an ear. Immediately Jesus turned to Peter with the command, "Put your sword back into its place; for all who take the sword will perish by the sword." (Matt. 26:52).

Peter and the brazier

The background of the incident of the two swords shows how important it is to examine the context and compare Scripture with Scripture. When we do this we discover that the more we dig the more we find. By digging even deeper into this tale of the two swords and two garments we find an interesting explanation of how Peter came to bring himself to the situation in which he denied his Master.

Although Peter was among those who fled after the arrest he nevertheless had the courage to follow Jesus to the palace of the high priest. Here, at the nerve centre of the Jewish administration, he found himself in a hostile and dangerous environment. Luke tells us that Peter followed afar off, but later we find him sitting among those warming themselves around the brazier. Here in the light of the fire he was recognized by the maid who had let him through the door (Mark 14:66-67). After being recognized and denying his Master, Peter realized the danger of exposing

---

1. Some have suggested that Jesus was saying that two swords were enough. But in the Greek, both the adjective *hikanon* (enough) and the verb *esti* (it is) are singular. They cannot possibly be translated 'they are enough'.

himself to the firelight and went out into the shadow of the porch (v.68), but for some reason he was drawn back to the fire: John tells us that when challenged the second time he was again warming himself (John 18:25). What was it that drew Peter back into the dangerous light of the brazier? It would seem that for an inadequately clothed Peter, who had sold his cloak, the imperative of keeping warm on a dark and cold winter morning overcame his fear of being recognized.

This tale of two swords again illustrates the supreme importance of recognizing figures of speech and the dangers of always taking the Bible literally. This incident is perhaps the commonest quoted by Christians to justify the use of armed force and yet it teaches the opposite!

Irony is frequently an expression of exasperation. The complete failure of the disciples to understand the sacrificial mission of Jesus brought forth the ironic rebuke that they should buy swords. Later that day when his chosen three disciples failed to support him in his Gethsemane vigil, Jesus again rebuked them with irony. They had fallen asleep for the third time, and as he was about to be arrested, Jesus said,

> **Sleep on now and take your rest: behold the hour is at hand, and the Son of man is betrayed into the hands of sinners. Matt. 26:45 KJV**

The KJV, true to its policy of literal translation, has preserved the sad ironic imperative. But it has been lost by the RSV, NKJV and later versions with their paraphrase, "Are you still sleeping and taking your rest?"

CHAPTER 25

THE UNJUST STEWARD AND THE RICH MAN AND LAZARUS

In Luke 16 we have two parables concerning the misuse of riches (mammon) which are regarded as difficult but which can be better understood once we have grasped the relevance of irony.

> 1. And he said also unto his disciples, There was a certain rich man, which had a steward; and the same was accused unto him that he had wasted his goods.
> 2. And he called him, and said unto him, How is it that I hear this of thee? give an account of thy stewardship; for thou mayest be no longer steward.
> 3. Then the steward said within himself, What shall I do? for my lord taketh away from me the stewardship: I cannot dig; to beg I am ashamed.
> 4. I am resolved what to do, that, when I am put out of the stewardship, they may receive me into their houses.
> 5. So he called every one of his lord's debtors unto him, and said unto the first, How much owest thou unto my lord?
> 6. And he said, An hundred measures of oil. And he said unto him, Take thy bill, and sit down quickly, and write fifty.
> 7. Then said he to another, And how much owest thou? And he said, An hundred measures of wheat. And he said unto him, Take thy bill, and write fourscore.
> 8. And the lord commended the unjust steward, because he had done wisely: for the children of this world are in their generation wiser than the children of light.
> 9. And I say unto you, Make to yourselves friends of the mammon of unrighteousness; that, when ye fail, they may receive you into everlasting habitations.
> 10. He that is faithful in that which is least is faithful also in much: and he that is unjust in the least is unjust also in much.   Luke 16:1-10   KJV

This parable of the Unjust Steward is the story of an unscrupulous business manager who, faced with dismissal for embezzlement, reduced the debts of his employer's customers in order to gain their support after losing his job. Up to verse 7 it is a straightforward story of a clever swindler. But then in verse 8 the parable ends with a strange twist — the employer commends the unjust steward. More surprisingly in the next verse Jesus then appears to be advising his hearers to follow the steward's example.

In the first half of verse 8 we see that "the master commended the unjust steward because he had dealt shrewdly". This was ironic. He was not commending the steward for being a swindler; he was commending his shrewdness in preparing for his future. He was saying in effect, "Although I am dismissing you I must admit that you are a clever rogue."

The parable ends here and in the second half of verse 8 Jesus began his commentary on the parable. To understand this we need to know to whom Jesus was speaking. Verse 1 tells us that he was addressing his disciples, but verse 14 informs us that the Pharisees were listening. His audience was divided and so were his comments. He began by saying, "For the sons of this world are more shrewd in their generation than the sons of light." Here Jesus was addressing the disciples and explaining that the lesson in the parable for them was that worldly people make better provision for their future in this life than godly people do for their eternal future.

Now we come to the extraordinary statement in verse 9 where Jesus said,

> **And I say unto you, Make to yourselves friends of the mammon of unrighteousness; that, when ye fail, they may receive you into everlasting habitations.**

The suggestion that they should use unrighteous wealth to make provision for their future could not apply to his disciples because they had no money. They had given up their livelihoods. Jesus had told them to carry no money (Matt. 10:9) and their meagre requirements were purchased from a money bag held by a thief (John 12:6). It is therefore evident that in verse 9 Jesus had turned his gaze upon the other half of his audience and with piercing irony was accusing the Pharisees of behaving like the Unjust Steward. He said, in effect, "And I tell *you*, carry on with your dishonest religious practices and when you die you will receive an eternal reward!"

The Pharisees would have understood the irony. In verse 14 the listening Pharisees were described as 'lovers of money' (Gk. *philarguros*) and we know from Luke 20:47 that they 'devoured widows' houses' and for a pretence made long prayers.

Thus the main thrust of this parable was directed at the money-loving Jewish clerics who were defrauding their divine Master. They were pretending to uphold the Law but were serving mammon which they hoped would ensure them a secure future.

In the original Greek, 'habitations' is *skēnas* which means tents. This reference to everlasting tents was deliberate and ironic. It was almost certainly a reference to the Jewish myth that the righteous would end up in 'Abraham's bosom'. As Heb. 11:9 reminds us, Abraham was the archetypal tent-dweller who never built a permanent dwelling. And as we shall see, Jesus made direct reference to Abraham's bosom in the next parable which is closely related to this one.

Stung by the lesson of the parable the Pharisees derided Jesus. But Jesus reminded them of the message of John the Baptist who, like the rich man in the parable, had given notice of their dismissal (verse 16) when he warned them that the axe was laid at the root of their tree (Luke 3:9). Jesus then asserted that God's law, which they were mishandling, would be fulfilled and as an example of how they were perverting God's law he re-affirmed the law of divorce (verse 18). He chose this example because this was an area where the Jewish clerics were growing rich by selling 'bills of divorcement' on almost any pretext for the appropriate fee.[1] Like the unjust steward they were issuing false documents.

Immediately after this Jesus continued the theme by addressing a parable directly to the Pharisees in which he condemned their ostentatious wealth, their lack of concern for the poor and their failure to heed Moses and the Prophets.

This parable tells of a very rich man at whose gate a beggar named Lazarus used to sit. Both died. The beggar is carried to Abraham's bosom and the rich man to Hades where he is tortured by fire. Across the gulf between them a conversation takes place.

Although Jesus appears to be accepting the Jewish myths on which the story is based, a study of the parable will reveal that it is profoundly ironic. Jesus used their myths as a basis for driving home some very powerful lessons and in the process he demonstrated the absurdity of their beliefs.

Under the influence of their Babylonian and Persian conquerors in the four hundred years between the Old and New Testaments, the Jews came to believe in the immortality of the soul and this meant they they had to find a place for souls after death. Souls went into a dark underworld called Hades. From there the righteous were led to a region of light, a garden of Eden in heaven, called 'Abraham's bosom' in the Talmud, where Abraham is depicted standing as a warden at the gate of Paradise to receive and embrace his children as they enter. The wicked, on the other hand, were banished to a lake of fire in Hades from where they could see the righteous across an impassable gulf.

---

1. According to Hillel a man could sue for divorce if his wife put too much salt in his soup!

The lesson of this parable is contained in the last verse. The parable is a bitter condemnation of the Pharisees who, by their way of life, flouted the true spirit of the Law of Moses. At the end of his ministry Jesus raised Lazarus, the brother of Mary and Martha, from the dead. The response of the priests and Pharisees was to seek to kill Jesus (John 11:53) and also to get rid of the evidence by killing Lazarus (John 12:10).

So in spite of having witnessed this wonderful miracle of the raising of Lazarus they refused to be persuaded and remained unconverted. Hence the appropriateness of the words of Abraham in the last verse, "If they do not listen to Moses and the Prophets, neither will they be convinced even if someone rises from the dead."

By employing the Jewish myths of Paradise and Hades as the basis of the parable Jesus effectively mocked their beliefs. Thus there is a conversation across the divide between heaven and hell in which the rich man asks if Lazarus could come over and dip his finger in water and cool his tongue! He then asks if Lazarus would go and warn his five brothers — an allusion to the fact that Caiaphas the high priest had five brothers-in-law who held high priestly office at one time or another.

This parable was addressed to intelligent and educated men. We are not told how they reacted, but we can be sure that they would not have failed to detect the subtle irony of the parable. How tragic then that it should be used to support the blasphemous doctrine of eternal torment!

CHAPTER 26

CONCESSION

Jesus' apparent acceptance of the Jewish myth of Abraham's bosom is an example of a figure of speech known as concession (or argumentum ex concessis or synchoresis). In this figure of speech (not to be confused with 'condescension' in Ch.21) a false premise is accepted in order to demolish it. In other words, ground is conceded in order to beat an opponent on his own ground. A simple example is found in Luke 19:22 in the parable of the nobleman. The servant who had been given one pound to trade failed to put the money to use and excused himself by saying, "... for I was afraid of you, because you are a harsh man; you take what you did not deposit, and reap what you did not sow." In the parable, the nobleman, who represents Jesus, replies,

> **I will judge you by your own words, you wicked slave! You knew, did you, that I was a harsh man, taking what I did not deposit and reaping what I did not sow? Why then did you not put my money into the bank? Then when I returned, I could have collected it with interest. Luke 19:22-23 NRSV**

Here Jesus is apparently acknowledging that he is a hard business man. But he does so in order to condemn the idle servant *out of his own mouth*.

Another example of concession is the way Jesus appeared to accept the Jewish myth of Beelzebub as the prince of demons. When confronted with the absurd accusation that he was casting out demons by the power of Beelzebub, the prince of demons, Jesus could have answered in one of two ways. He could have said, "There is no such power as Beelzebub; he doesn't exist." But he chose the more subtle approach saying,

> If I cast out demons by Beelzebub, by whom do your sons cast them out?[1] Therefore they shall be your judges. But if I cast out demons by the Spirit of God, surely the kingdom of God has come upon you."
> Matt. 12:27,28

By conceding the possible existence of their god of demons Jesus showed that their accusation was absurdly illogical and his ability to 'cast out demons' proved that he was in full control of their demon god.

Legion

A further example of concession is found in the way Jesus dealt with Legion, a man who claimed to be possessed by many demons (Luke 8:26). Instead of trying to persuade the man that he was suffering from a mental illness he appears to accept that this was a case of multiple demon possession and then proceeded to demonstrate that he was in control of their demons. And by agreeing to cast them into swine he taught a powerful lesson to those who were openly flouting the Law of Moses by farming 'unclean' animals.

It appears, however, that Jesus sometimes spoke of demons as if they existed, in circumstances where he had no particular reason to give credence to popular beliefs. But again we have to ask what would have been the most effective way of dealing with their belief that certain diseases were caused by demons. Should Jesus have argued against it? Scientific explanations would have been met with incredulity and would have been a distraction from his mission to preach the gospel of the Kingdom of God. So he took the alternative course of using their classification of disease and demonstrated that, whatever the cause, he had power to heal and this power to heal was the evidence of his divine authority to forgive sins (Mark 2:10,11).

Further discussion of the N.T. classification of disease will be found in chapter 30 dealing with personification.

---

1. This is evidently an ironic reference to some followers of the Pharisees who practised exorcism but had obviously failed to cure this blind and dumb man.

CHAPTER 27

HYPERBOLE

This is a figure of speech in which there is deliberate exaggeration for the purpose of emphasis. An example in the Old Testament is found in Deut. 1:28,

> ... Our brethren have discouraged our hearts, saying, "The people are greater and taller than we; the cities are great and fortified up to heaven; moreover we have seen the sons of the Anakim there"

An example in the N.T. is found in the last verse of the Gospel of John where we read,

> But there are also many other things that Jesus did; if every one of them were written down, I suppose that the world itself could not contain the books that would be written. **NRSV**

Hyperbole is often combined with metaphor as in Matt. 7:3: "And why do you look at the speck in your brother's eye, but do not consider the plank in your own eye?" and in Matt. 23:24, "You blind guides! You strain out a gnat and swallow a camel!"

Important examples of hyperbolic metaphor are found in 2 Pet.3:10,

> But the day of the Lord will come as a thief in the night; in the which the heavens shall pass away with a great noise, and the elements shall melt with fervent heat, the earth also and the works that are therein shall be burned up. **KJV**

On the basis of this verse some Christians believe that our earth will eventually be destroyed by fire. But if we compare Scripture with Scripture we find that similar words were used by Peter on the day of Pentecost:

> **And I will show wonders in the heaven above, and signs in the earth beneath: blood, and fire and vapour of smoke. The sun shall be turned into darkness, and the moon into blood, before that great and notable day of the Lord come. Acts 2:19,20 KJV**

In this passage Peter is quoting directly from Joel 2:30-32 and in verse 16 Peter tells us that Joel was speaking about the coming of the Holy Spirit at Pentecost.[1] None would suggest that these words should be understood literally. Although there was the appearance of 'cloven tongues as of fire' there was no smoke nor was the moon turned into blood!

As we have seen in Ch. 20, Peter in his second epistle is predicting an even more dramatic event — the end of the Jewish state in AD 70. It is therefore appropriate that he should use even more powerful metaphors to describe this shattering event in which the Jewish political heavens would 'pass away' in the fiery heat of God's judgements.

These dramatic metaphors are not new — they are taken from the Old Testament. As we have seen 'heavens' is a metaphor for ruling powers (Isa. 1:2,10), 'earth' stands for people (Jer. 51:48) and 'fire' is used for God's judgement on the wicked (Mal. 4:1).

There are many plain passages of Scripture which negate the theory that the earth will be destroyed by fire, such as Num. 14:21 (repeated in Hab. 2:14 and Isa. 11:9) and especially Isa. 45:18,

> **For thus saith the LORD that created the heavens; God himself that formed the earth and made it; he hath established it, he created it not in vain, he formed it to be inhabited: I am the LORD: and there is none else. KJV**

---

1. Doubtless Joel's prophecy as it continues in Ch. 3 applies to even more dramatic future events.

God will not destroy the earth; on the contrary He will "destroy those who destroy the earth" (Rev. 11:18).

Although hyperbole is rare in prose writing it is very common in poetry, especially in Biblical poetry, and will be discussed further when we consider the importance of recognizing poetry in interpreting the Bible.

CHAPTER 28

UNIVERSALIST LANGUAGE

When Jeremiah prophesied the doom of "all kingdoms of the world which are on the face of the earth" (Jer 25:26) we would be wrong to assume that this was another example of hyperbole. It is universalist language. This prophecy can only be understood in relation to the context, and to the world of Jeremiah's day. Thus in verse 17 we read, "So I took the cup from the LORD'S hand, and made all the nations *to whom the LORD had sent me* drink it". We are then given a list of these nations: Egypt, Philistia, Edom, Moab, Ammon, Tyre, Sidon, Arabia and Persia. Then in verse 26 they are summed up as 'all the kings of the north, far and near, one after another, and all the kingdoms of the world that are on the face of the earth'. So 'all the kingdoms of the world' means all the nations in the area which we now describe as the Middle East.

There are many other examples of universalist language in Scripture. For example, Jesus said,

> **The queen of the South will rise up at the judgement with the people of this generation and condemn them, because she came from the ends of the earth to listen to the wisdom of Solomon, and see, something greater than Solomon is here! Matt. 12:42 NRSV**

In the time of our Lord, Sheba (Ethiopia) was regarded as the 'ends of the earth'.

Similarly, when we read in Luke 2:1 that in the time of Caesar Augustus *'all the world'* should be registered, and in Acts 11:28 that there would be 'a severe famine over *all the world'* in the days of Claudius, we understand that this referred to the Roman Empire. Similar examples of universalism are found in Gen. 41:56 and Dan. 4:22.

The Flood

This Scriptural use of universalist language is relevant to our understanding of the extent of Noah's flood. In Gen. 7:19-21 we read,

> The waters swelled so mightily on the earth that all the high mountains under the whole heaven were covered; the waters swelled above the mountains, covering them fifteen cubits deep. And all flesh died that moved on the earth, birds, domestic animals, wild animals, all swarming creatures that swarm on the earth, and all human beings. **NRSV**

Widely differing opinions prevail as to the extent of Noah's flood, but one thing must be made clear; we cannot use these verses to *prove* that the flood must have covered the whole globe. The Hebrew word for earth (*erets*) could mean the whole globe as in Gen. 1:1, "In the beginning God created the heavens and the earth." On the other hand it could mean a limited part of the earth as in 2 Chr. 36:23 where Cyrus, king of Persia, said, "The LORD, the God of heaven, has given me all the kingdoms of the earth."

The expression 'under the whole heaven' may appear comprehensive, but again it must be understood in the context. 'Under heaven' is a Bible idiom for man's domain, as in Acts 2:5, "Now there were devout Jews from every nation under heaven living in Jerusalem", and in Col. 1:23 '... the gospel that you heard, which has been proclaimed to every creature under heaven ...'. 'Under heaven' in these verses obviously relates only to the Roman Empire.

Also in Deut. 2:25 God said through Moses,

> This day will I begin to put the dread of thee and the fear of thee upon the nations that are under the whole heaven, who shall hear report of thee, and shall tremble, and be in anguish because of thee. **KJV**

The nations that are 'under the whole heaven' clearly refer to all those nations who had contact with Israel; America, China and Australia would not be included.

Similarly, in Gen. 7:19 the 'whole heaven' presumably refers to the whole area inhabited by wicked men at the time of the flood. We do not know the extent of this territory, but whatever its extent Gen. 7:17-22 makes it abundantly clear that over this area the earth was completely inundated and all life perished. This passage relates to the completeness of the flood rather than to its geographical extent. The emphasis is on the fact that all the high hills in the flooded area were covered.

Of course it is possible to interpret these verses as indicating that the flood was global and covered the whole surface of the earth. And this would be true if it could be proved that by this time Adam's posterity had spread over the whole surface of the earth. But the point we are making here is that any theory regarding the extent of the flood cannot be built on these verses alone.

In our opinion a global deluge is difficult to reconcile with the Biblical account of the flood because, with the vast preponderance of salt water in the oceans (about 35 times more salt water than fresh water), a global flood would have destroyed not only all terrestrial plants and habitats but also all freshwater fish and freshwater animals and plants. And yet there was no provision in the ark for the preservation of terrestrial plants or freshwater plants and animals. So how would they have survived in a global flood?

We readily accept that nothing is impossible with God and that He could have re-created all freshwater life and all the terrestrial habitats. But there is no hint of a new creation after the flood and if such a stupendous re-creation did occur, why was it necessary to preserve the land animals in the ark?[1]

Proponents of a global flood could ask: Why, if the flood were not worldwide, was it necessary to preserve species which could have been replaced by migration from unflooded areas? One answer is that the animals preserved in the ark were those of the region that was flooded and the purpose of their preservation was to restore the original ecological balance.

2 Pet. 3:5,6 is often quoted to support the concept of a global flood:

> **They deliberately ignore this fact, that by the word of God the heavens existed long ago and an earth *(gē)* was formed out of water and by means of water, through which the world *(kosmos)* of that time was deluged with water and perished. NRSV**

---

1. Robert Roberts in *The Visible Hand of God* writes, "The ways of God are always most wisely adapted to the requirements of each situation as it arises, and it will be found in the study of each case that the amount of miracle employed is the smallest that is called for. There is none of the prodigality of marvel — meaningless marvel that characterises all artificial histories — such as the Apocryphal Gospels, the Life of Mahomet or the Arabian Night Entertainments ... It would have been easy for God to have isolated a certain district from which the destroying waters should have been kept, and within which Noah and all his would have been protected from the destroying tempest. Instead of that, just as the death of the doomed population was effected by natural means, so the salvation of Noah was effected by natural means, by the floating of a wooden structure within which he had previously retired for safety ... Considering the comparatively limited extent of the human family at the time, and that it was confined to one small district of the globe, it would seem reasonable to conclude that the Flood was coextensive only with the Adamically-inhabited portion of the globe." *The Visible Hand of God* (1883) Reprint obtainable from: The Christadelphian, 404 Shaftmoor Lane, Birmingham B28 8SZ.

We note that in this statement Peter deliberately uses two different Greek words. First there is *gē* which means the literal earth. Then he uses *kosmos* which means 'world order' and commonly refers to abstract concepts such as political or social orders. This accords with his words in the previous chapter where Peter tells us that God brought in the flood upon the world (*kosmos*) of the ungodly (2 Pet. 2:5). The analogy is that of the literal earth being created *out of water* (Gen. 1:9) and the social order being destroyed *by water.*

CHAPTER 29

PERSONIFICATION

This is a figure of speech in which personality is given to an abstract quality. For example, in Prov. 8 wisdom is described as a virtuous woman who cries at the gates of the city and speaks of 'excellent things'.

The most sustained and important example of personification in the Bible is the use of satan and the devil. Satan is an untranslated Hebrew word meaning adversary. Devil is a translation of a Greek word *diabolos* which means slanderer. The O.T. only uses satan whereas the N.T. uses both diabolos and satan.

Satan in the Old Testament

Satan is an ordinary Hebrew word which means an adversary of one kind or another. But when it is personified by the use of the definite article (the Satan) it is wrongly assumed that it refers to an evil demi-god or fallen angel.

A typical example of the ordinary use of *satan* in the O.T. is found in 1 Kin. 11:14:

> **Now the LORD raised up an adversary (*satan*) against Solomon, Hadad the Edomite.**

In Num. 22:21-22 the adversary is an angel of the LORD:

> **And Balaam rose up in the morning and saddled his ass and went with the princes of Moab. And God's anger was kindled because he went: and the angel of the LORD stood in the way for an adversary (*satan*) against him. KJV**

God as a Satan

A very revealing example of the use of *satan* is in 1 Chr. 21:1,

> Now Satan stood up against Israel and moved David to number Israel.

Hebrew has no indefinite article and since in this verse there is no definite article *satan* should have been translated 'an adversary'. Who then was the adversary in this statement? We are left in no doubt on reading the parallel account of the same incident in 2 Sam. 24:1,

> **Again the anger of the LORD was kindled against Israel, and He moved David against them to say, 'Go number Israel and Judah'. KJV**

So the adversary in 1 Chr. 21:1 was none other than God Himself. God was acting as an adversary to punish a wicked nation.

There are only two passages in the O.T. where *satan* is personified by the use of the definite article. These are in Zech. 3 and Job 1 and 2.

The Samaritan Satan

In Zech. 3 we have a dramatized vision in which Satan is one of the actors.

> **And he shewed me Joshua the high priest standing before the angel of the LORD, and Satan standing at his right hand to resist him. And the LORD said unto Satan, The LORD rebuke thee, O Satan; even the LORD that hath chosen Jerusalem rebuke thee: is not this a brand plucked out of the fire? Now Joshua was clothed with filthy garments, and stood before the angel. And he answered and spake unto those that stood before him, saying, Take away the filthy garments from him. And unto him he said, Behold, I have caused thine iniquity to pass from thee, and I will clothe thee with change of raiment. KJV**

This symbolic vision can only be understood by comparing Scripture with Scripture. Zechariah and Haggai were the two prophets whose role was to encourage the rebuilding of the temple by Joshua and Zerubbabel after the return of the Jews from 70 years' captivity in Babylon. In this little drama there was an adversary called Satan who was rebuked and Joshua the High Priest who was cleansed. Satan represented the Samaritan adversaries who succeeded in halting the building of the temple, as described in Ezra 4. Two years later building was resumed under the influence of the prophets Haggai and Zechariah but the builders were again opposed by the Samaritans. However, following an appeal to Darius, the Samaritans were severely rebuked and the temple was completed. It is relevant that in this vision the LORD told Satan that *Jerusalem* was the chosen place for the temple — a refutation of the Samaritan claim that the temple should be built on Gerizim (cf. John 4:20).

Why did Joshua need to be cleansed from his 'filthy garments'? Joshua was the High Priest and as such he represented the people (Lev. 16:34) who had become 'unclean' (Hag. 2:14). So we read that at the dedication of the temple, "the priests and the Levites were purified together ... and the children of Israel had separated themselves from the *filthiness* of the heathen" (Ezra 6:20,21).

In verse 9 of his epistle Jude refers to this incident:

> **Yet Michael the archangel, in contending with the devil when he disputed about the body of Moses, dared not bring against him a reviling accusation, but said, "The Lord rebuke you."**

This informs us that the angel in Zech. 3 was Michael whom Daniel described as the guardian of the children of Israel (Dan. 12:1). The 'body of Moses' represented the people of Israel who had been 'baptized into Moses' (1 Cor. 10:2) just as the 'body of Christ' represents those who have been baptized into Christ. Jude calls the Samaritan adversaries 'the devil' which is identified with Satan (Rev. 12:9). There are further echoes of Zech. 3 in Jude 23 referring to 'garment spotted by the flesh' and 'pulled out of the fire'.

The parallels between Zech. 3 and Jude are so striking (Table 1) that there is no doubt that they refer to the same vision — a vision which illustrates the consistent meaning of satan as an adversary of one kind or another but never the demon-god of pagan mythology.

Zechariah Ch. 3	Jude
Joshua the High Priest	The body of Moses
Satan	The devil
The Angel of the LORD	Michael the archangel
"The LORD rebuke thee"	"The LORD rebuke thee"
Filthy garments	Garment spotted by the flesh
A brand plucked out of the fire	Pulling them out of the fire

Table 1　Parallels between Zechariah 3 and Jude

Job's adversary

The only other O.T. personification of *satan* occurs in the first two chapters of Job. Of one thing we can be certain: the Satan of Job does not correspond to the Satan of popular theology. Job's Satan converses in a friendly way with God who gives him the power to test Job by afflicting him (see 1:12 and 2:6).

As we shall show (Ch.35), the structure and language of the book of Job show that it is a highly stylized drama written in strict poetical form. So it is not surprising to find that the prologue written in prose uses figurative language. The prologue presents us with a picture of a heavenly court where Job's adversary (Satan) suggests to God that Job was righteous, only because he prospered and enjoyed good health. Who could have made such a suggestion? We find the answer by following the rule that Scripture interprets Scripture. In the drama Eliphaz, one of Job's three 'friends' (friends is ironic), levels the same charges against Job as Satan does in the prologue (4:4,5). Moreover, later in the chapter, Job rails against his miserable 'comforters' and then makes this complaint,

> **God has delivered me to the ungodly, And turned me over to the hands of the wicked. Job 16:11**

The implication of this verse is clear. Since the prologue tells us that it was God who had delivered Job into the hand of Satan, then the Satan in the prologue is none other than a personification of Job's three 'friends'. It therefore seems likely that the book of Job is based on the actual experience of a man who was tested by jealous friends. In contrast to their despicable accusations Job showed his magnanimity by praying for their forgiveness (Job 42:8-10).

Of course the drama of Job is much more than a story of human jealousy; it is a divinely inspired commentary on the problem of suffering. The dramatic structure of the book will be discussed in Ch.35.

A Fallen Angel?

A passage in Isa. 14 is frequently quoted to support the theory that Satan is a rebellious angel who was expelled from heaven:

> **How art thou fallen from heaven, O Lucifer, son of the morning! how art thou cut down to the ground, which didst weaken the nations! For thou hast said in thine heart, I will ascend into the heaven, I will exalt my throne above the stars of God; I will sit also upon the mount of the congregation, in the sides of the north. Isa. 14:12,13 KJV**

Apart from the fact that Satan is not mentioned here, if we look at the context we see that this passage is part of a long prophecy against Babylon, commencing in Ch.13, where the extinction of the power of Babylon is likened to the darkening of the sun, moon and stars (v.10).

The metaphorical use of the heavenly bodies to depict the fall of Babylon is elaborated in this passage where the king of Babylon is likened to the brightest star falling from heaven. Any doubt as to the identity of Lucifer is dispelled in verse 16 where those who witnessed the fall the Babylon exclaimed, "Is this the *man* who made the earth tremble, who shook kingdoms ...?"

There is no reason to regard Lucifer as a fallen angel who roams the world seeking to lead men into sin. The context of the passage makes it abundantly clear that Lucifer is a personification of the king of Babylon whose 'star' was about to fall from the political 'heavens'. But in spite of its obvious allusion to Babylon many people argue that the fall of Lucifer also refers to a literal event in heaven when Satan led a rebellion among the angelic host that led to his expulsion from heaven, after which he sought to frustrate the purpose of God by introducing evil into God's creation. This interpretation of the prophecy against Babylon is redolent of pagan dualism and is not supported by Scripture.[1]

Conclusion

In the O.T. *satan* is an ordinary Hebrew word meaning adversary. When used with the definite article *satan* is personified but it never refers to an evil demi-god.

---

1. Jude 6 is alleged to refer to the fall of Satan but the previous verse indicates that the angels were those who rebelled after the exodus from Egypt and v.11 identifies this rebellion as that of Korah and his followers (Num. 16). The Hebrew and Greek words translated 'angel' may also refer to human agents e.g. Gen. 32:3 and Luke 7:24.

CHAPTER 30

SATAN AND DEVIL IN THE NEW TESTAMENT

The few examples of personification of satan in the O.T. contrast with the N.T. where satan is always personified and the devil is often personified. The reason for this difference will be found in the 430 year gap between the Testaments. When Isaiah prophesied that Cyrus would allow the captive Jews to return from Babylon to Israel, he added this solemn declaration:

> **I am the LORD and there is none else, there is no God beside me .... I form the light and create darkness: I make peace and create evil:[1] I the LORD do all these things. Isa. 45:5-7 KJV**

This was a very important message for the returning captives because they would have been exposed for 70 years to pagan dualism with its gods of good and gods of evil, constantly at war with each other.[2] Sadly, Isaiah's warning was not heeded. In the years between the Testaments the Jews continued to absorb the mythology of their Persian and later their Greek overlords so that by N.T. times they were capable of the ultimate blasphemy of attributing the miracles of Jesus to Beelzebub the 'ruler of the demons' (Matt. 12:24). This change is evident in the Jewish apocryphal writings between the testaments. These books abound with references to spirits, angels and demons. And it is significant that the demon in the Book of Tobit has a Persian name, Asmodaeus. The change from strict monotheism to dualism caused a profound change in

---

1. The Hebrew word *ra*, translated 'evil', can refer to unfavourable events, rather than moral evil, so the NKJV has 'calamity'.

2. In the Persian holy book, Ormuzd was the god of good spirits and Ahriman was the god of evil spirits, the latter being responsible for disease, death, evil beasts, etc.

the figures of speech of everyday language so that evil influences were personified in such terms as Satan (Acts 5:3), the devil (Heb. 2:14), the prince of this world (Eph. 2:2), the dragon (Rev. 20:2), the rulers of darkness (Eph. 6:12), etc.

It would be a great mistake to suppose that the use of such terms by N.T. writers implied their acceptance of the underlying pagan philosophy. We can talk of lunatics without believing that such people are moonstruck. Nor do we imply a belief in demon possession when we speak of pandemonium.

N.T. medical terminology

In N.T. times evil spirits were regarded as responsible for diseases for which there was no visible cause. Thus in Matt. 9:27 two men are described simply as 'blind men' because their eyes were visibly diseased, but shortly afterwards Jesus encountered a dumb man who was said to be possessed by a devil. In this case there would be no apparent cause for his inability to speak, so his affliction was attributed to a supernatural power. In this way pagan concepts of dualism influenced the medical language of N.T. times.

It was natural for Jesus to speak in the idiom of his day. So in Matt. 10:8 Jesus told his disciples to "Heal the sick, cleanse the lepers, raise the dead, cast out demons ..." This does not imply that Jesus believed that leprosy was cured by 'cleansing' nor that mysterious illnesses were caused by demons. Jesus' use of conventional terms does not mean that he understood them literally — any more than we believe the sun is moving because we speak of 'sunrise'.

Another example of Jesus' use of conventional terms is found in Matt. 18:17,

> If he refuses to listen to them, tell it to the church; and if he refuses to listen even to the church, let him be to you as a Gentile and a tax collector. RSV

Here Jesus was using the words 'Gentile' and 'tax collector' as synonyms for 'outcasts' because these were the current Jewish idioms. It is inconceivable that Jesus would be subscribed to the view that tax collectors were outcasts — indeed we know that he consorted with them (Mark 2:15), compared them favourably with the religious leaders of his day (Matt 21:31) and chose a tax gatherer as one of his disciples (Matt. 9:9).

The N.T. meaning of devil and Satan

We should first note that devil and Satan are interchangeable:

> **And the great dragon was cast out, that old serpent called the Devil and Satan ... Rev. 12:9   KJV**

The terms are seen to have essentially the same meaning. Moreover since satan is a Hebrew O.T. word, it will have the same root meaning namely, 'adversary'. The Greek word *diabolos*, usually translated 'devil', is also translated 'false accuser' (2 Tim. 3:3 and Titus 2:3). So it has a very similar root meaning to the Hebrew word *satan*. Thus when we read in 2 Tim. 3:3 that in the last days men shall be "without natural affection, trucebreakers, false accusers *(diaboloi)*, incontinent, fierce, despisers of those that are good ..." we all agree that *diaboloi* applies to evil *men*. Difficulties arise when *diabolos* is personified and the figurative language is misunderstood and *diabolos* is applied to an evil demi-god.

The devil within

In John's gospel we have two references to Judas Iscariot showing how readily the N.T. switches from the literal to the figurative use of *diabolos*. Referring to Judas Iscariot, Jesus said, "Have not I chosen you twelve, and one of you is a devil?" (John 6:70). Here Jesus was using the word 'devil' literally; Judas was *a* devil because he was opposing the will of God. But not long afterwards John writes, "The devil had already put it into the heart of Judas, son of Simon Iscariot, to betray him."

(John 13:2). Here the evil in the heart of Judas is personified as *the* devil. Judas was motivated by *greed* (John 12:6), not by some outside evil power.

We see from this example that the N.T. 'devil' is essentially the indwelling spirit of rebellion which lies in the heart of all men. It is the 'natural man' (1 Cor. 2:14) which tends to follow the promptings of the 'flesh' (See Ch. 18).

The testimony of Jesus

In Mark 7:21-23 Jesus makes it clear that man alone is responsible for sin:

> **For from within, out of the heart of man, come evil thoughts, fornication, theft, murder, adultery, coveting, wickedness, deceit, licentiousness, envy, slander, pride, foolishness. All these evil things come from within and they defile a man. RSV**

There is no suggestion in this passage of a supernatural power enticing us to sin; sin is part of our nature.

However there were occasions in the N.T. when people prompted others to sin, as in Matt. 16:22 when Peter tempted Jesus with the attractive proposition that the crucifixion which he was about to suffer was not necessary. Jesus must have felt the force of this temptation and rebuked Peter with the words,

> **Get behind me, Satan! You are a stumbling-block to me; for you are setting your mind not on divine things but on human things. NRSV**

In this incident Peter was, in effect, challenging the declared will of God. There is no suggestion that Peter was being influenced by a malign power; he was expressing his own robust opinion based on human thinking. Here Peter was a satan or adversary to our Lord because he was rejecting God's plan of salvation; he was opposing the will of God.

Whenever satan or devil is personified in the Bible it refers to a *human* adversary.

An examination of other passages where devil and Satan are used in the N.T. reveals the same pattern. Jesus called the Pharisees sons of the devil when, in the face of clear evidence of his divine power, they denied his authority (John 8:44). In 1 Pet. 5:8 the adversary, or devil, is described as a "roaring lion looking for someone to devour" — a clear reference to the persecutors of the infant church.

The deceitfulness of human nature is alluded to in expressions such as 'snare of the devil' (1 Tim. 3:7) and 'wiles of the devil' (Eph. 6:11). These are appropriate metaphors for our remarkable capacity for self deception (Heb. 3:13). Paul's description of Satan as an 'angel of light' in 2 Cor. 11:14 is a clear reference back to Gen. 3:5 where the Serpent claimed privileged insight into God's mind.

The context always provides the best guide to the meaning of a word (Ch.2). This is especially true when we have two parallel passages one of which uses the obscure word and the other a straightforward word. Thus in Acts 5:3 Peter said to Ananias, "Why has Satan filled your heart to lie to the Holy Spirit ...?" Almost immediately he repeats the question, "How is it that you have contrived this deed in your heart?" It is therefore evident that "Satan filled your heart" means "contrived in your heart". There is no suggestion here that Ananias was prompted by a supernatural power of evil; the evil arose from within him.

From these examples in the N.T. it will be evident that **when the words devil and satan are personified they refer to man's opposition to the authority and will of God.**

The parable of the sower

In the parable of the sower Jesus provides us with a very clear insight into the meaning of the words 'devil' and 'Satan'. The three accounts in Matt. 13:3-23, Mark 4:3-23 and Luke 8:4-15 use 'wicked one', 'Satan' and 'devil' respectively, showing that the devil and Satan are interchangeable and bear the same meaning.

In this parable the seed, which is the word of God, falls on four kinds of ground: hard paths, shallow soil, weedy soil and good soil. Jesus himself interprets the parable. The hard ground of the wayside where the seed is immediately devoured by birds represents those who instantly reject the word of God. Shallow soil, which causes rapid germination followed by withering in the sun, represents those who lose faith in the face of persecution. Soil full of weeds which choke the plants represents those whose faith becomes smothered by worldly preoccupations. The fertile soil represents those who allow the word of God to bear fruit in their lives.

Jesus explains that the birds that devour the seed symbolize the devil or Satan. They represent the human challenge to God's word. This is the challenge that either denies God's existence or refuses to accept God's authority. It is important to note that the devil snatched away only the seed on the wayside which had not had time to germinate. The devil is not implicated in the fate of those who wither under persecution nor those who are choked by worldly pleasures. Jesus does not speak of the devil or Satan as responsible for sins of weakness. He uses these names to personify the most serious sin of all, human pride which rejects the authority of God's word.

The devil in the wilderness

The account of the temptation of Jesus Christ in the wilderness dramatically illustrates this role of the devil. Jesus had just been invested with divine power (Matt. 3:16) and the temptations all urged him to use this power for his own gratification and glory. In each case Jesus countered the temptations with an affirmation of the authority of God's word, based on quotations from the book of Deuteronomy.

We do not need to involve another person in this incident. Jesus shared our nature (Heb. 2:14) and was "in all points tempted as we are, yet without sin". The temptations could have arisen quite naturally and without any promptings from outside. The fact that in the third temptation the devil claimed to have sovereignty over 'all the kingdoms of the world' strongly suggests that the temptations came from within the mind of our Lord. Who else could claim such power? Did not Jesus declare that he had twelve legions of angels at his immediate call? (Matt. 26:53). It was his possession of this power that made the temptations so powerful. As we hope to show in chapter 35 the account of the temptation has a dramatic structure and as such it is appropriate that the impulses which Jesus overcame should be personified.

It is significant that after the wilderness temptations Luke tells us that the devil departed from Jesus 'for a season'. The pattern of the wilderness temptation was repeated throughout his life. It was in the garden of Gethsemane that he rendered his final and complete submission to the will of his Father (Luke 22:39-46). In the temptation of Jesus the history of Eden was re-enacted with Jesus, as the last Adam, succeeding where Adam and Eve had failed.

This brief survey of the origin of evil shows that our understanding of this contentious subject depends on our interpretation of Biblical language. Those who take the language literally see the problem of evil as a conflict between a righteous God and a wicked demi-god. We believe that the Bible strongly repudiates this pagan dualism. The only 'dualism' in the Bible is the conflict between God's law and man's rebellious nature. This is the conflict that began in Eden.

The Serpent in Eden

In Rev. 20:2 Jesus equates the devil and satan with the serpent in Eden:

> **And he laid hold on the dragon, that old serpent, which is the Devil, and Satan, and bound him a thousand years. KJV**

The serpent in Gen. 3 was described as "more cunning than any beast of the field which the LORD God had made." Although it was called the 'serpent' we are given no details about its appearance. Our only information is that it was subtle and had the power of speech. In popular imagination and in pictorial representations of the temptation, the serpent is depicted as a snake. But this cannot be right because the serpent was only condemned to go on its belly *after* the temptation. Thus the name 'serpent' was not a description of the physical appearance of the tempter. The name was given in order to emphasize the character of the tempter. It was a metaphor for the subtlety of sin. Similarly, when Jesus said of Herod, "Go tell that fox ..." he was giving Herod an appropriate name for a cunning and ruthless man.

The serpent personified the rebellion latent in the heart of Eve and in the hearts of all mankind. Jesus insisted that all forms of evil arise from within the human heart (Mark 7:21-23). So Adam and Eve represent all of us. The serpent in Eden is the prototype of both Satan and the devil. It represents the inherent tendency of man to deny God's authority and assert human autonomy.

There is therefore no justification for the popular dualistic concept of Adam and Eve as innocents into whose minds evil was injected by a wicked demigod or fallen angel. The serpent was a symbol of man's rebellious nature so it is appropriate that the curse on the serpent should be expressed in highly symbolic language and contain six different metaphors illustrating the nature of sin and its conquest:

> So the LORD God said to the serpent:
> "Because you have done this,
> You are cursed more than all cattle,
> And more than every beast of the field;
> On your belly you shall go,
> And you shall eat dust
> All the days of your life.
> And I will put enmity
> Between you and the woman,
> And between your seed and her Seed;
> He shall bruise your head,
> And you shall bruise his heel." Gen. 3:14,15

We shall briefly consider these metaphors.

1. *"On your belly you shall go":* Crawling on the belly symbolizes humiliation, as in Psa. 44:25,

   > For our soul is bowed down to the dust; our body clings to the ground.

2. *"You shall eat dust all the days of your life":* This clearly cannot be literal because snakes do not eat dust; they are all carnivorous and eat small animals, insects, eggs etc. Eating dust is a metaphor signifying humiliation as in Psa. 72:9,

   > May his foes bow down before him, and his enemies lick the dust! NRSV

3. *"I will put enmity between you and the woman":* This refers to the age-long conflict between sin, represented by the serpent, and mankind, represented by the woman.

4. *"... and between your (the serpent's) seed and her (the woman's) seed":* This and the two following statements foreshadow the work of the Messiah. The seed of the woman is Jesus Christ who was born of a woman, without the aid of a man. The seed of the serpent

refers to the sinners who opposed Jesus and his ministry. We remember the words of Jesus to his enemies, "You snakes, you brood of vipers! How can you escape being sentenced to hell?" (Matt. 23:33).

5. *"He (the seed of the woman) will strike your (the serpent's) head":* This depicts Jesus mortally wounding the power of sin by a fatal head injury. This victory is described in Heb. 2:14:

> **Since, therefore, the children share flesh and blood, he himself likewise shared the same things, so that through death he might destroy the one who has the power of death, that is, the devil. NRSV**

Jesus slew the serpent by sharing our sin-tending nature (but never yielding to it) and then allowing it to be destroyed on the cross.

6. *"You (the serpent) will strike his (Jesus Christ's) heel":* Although Jesus Christ had a mortal body (Heb. 2:14) he died because he was executed by men whom he called 'serpents' (Matt. 23:33). But the grave could not hold him because he was "holy, harmless and undefiled and separate from sinners" (Heb. 7:26).

In John 3:14-15 we have a very interesting reference to the serpent which reinforces the teaching of Heb. 2:14:

> **And as Moses lifted up the serpent in the wilderness, even so must the Son of man be lifted up, that whosoever believeth in him should not perish but have eternal life. KJV**

How does a brass serpent on a pole represent the crucified Saviour? Just as the sinful Israelites who had been bitten by serpents were saved by looking on the brazen serpent so those who have been poisoned by the 'sting of death' (1 Cor. 15:56) will be saved by "looking unto Jesus the author and finisher of our faith" (Heb.12:2). And if the serpent represents the impulses to rebellion which are part of our animal nature then a serpent transfixed on a pole is an appropriate symbol of the conquest of that nature which Jesus accomplished by his sinless life and sacrificial death.

The destruction of the devil and Satan

Jesus crushed the head of the serpent which means that he mortally wounded the devil and Satan. This is explained in a highly significant statement in Heb. 2:14:

> **Forasmuch then as the children are partakers of flesh and blood, he also himself likewise took part of the same; that through death he might destroy him that had the power of death, that is, the devil. KJV**

This verse provides the most striking evidence that the devil cannot be a supernatural god of evil. How could the fact that Jesus had our flesh and blood have enabled him to destroy a powerful demi-god? And how could the *death* of Jesus destroy such a powerful opponent? But if the devil personifies the rebellious tendencies within human nature then the verse makes sense. Jesus destroyed the devil by his death because the crucifixion was the fulfilment of a life of total submission to the will of his Father. The crucifixion symbolized the completion of the conquest of sin and the triumph of good over evil. The only perfect man who ever lived had destroyed the power of sin in his human nature, and had thus destroyed the devil. In spite of inheriting our flesh and blood he was "holy, harmless, undefiled and separate from sinners" (Heb. 7:26).

It is the infinite privilege of the followers of Jesus to share in his victory over the devil. This we can do by taking up our cross (self-denial), confessing our sins, following him into the grave by baptism (Rom. 6:4) and being redeemed by his sacrificial death.

CHAPTER 31

ELLIPSIS

Another example of a figure of speech which can lead to misunderstanding is ellipsis which means putting a part for the whole (an ellipse being a partial circle). An elliptical statement is incomplete because a word or words have been omitted for the sake of brevity. A simple example of ellipsis is found in Mark 10:23,24:

> **Then Jesus looked around and said to his disciples, "How hard it is for those who have riches to enter the kingdom of God!"**

When his disciples expressed astonishment at his words Jesus showed that he was speaking elliptically by using a different verb:

> **And the disciples were astonished at his words. But Jesus answered again and said to them: "Children, how hard it is for those who *trust* in riches to enter the kingdom of God!"**

A more subtle example of ellipsis occurs in Gal. 5:2 where Paul writes:

> **Listen! I, Paul, am telling you that if you let yourselves be circumcised, Christ will be of no benefit to you. NRSV**

Clearly Paul is not saying that it is wrong to be circumcised. What he means is that if you are circumcised, *with the idea that this will confer some special privilege*, then you have failed to understand that salvation is not by works but by grace.

Eye for Eye

Ellipsis is a very common figure of speech because it is a form of verbal shorthand. Shortening a sentence increases the impact; it creates a short, sharp shock which drives home a lesson. But unless it is recognized it can easily be misunderstood. For example, the Law of Moses is frequently regarded as a brutal law on the basis of Exod. 21:24 where we read, "Eye for eye, tooth for tooth, hand for hand, foot for foot." It is often assumed that this means that if someone knocks out your teeth you can do the same to him.

This interpretation completely ignores the context which relates to harm done to a pregnant woman. The full text reads,

> **When people who are fighting injure a pregnant woman so that there is a miscarriage, and yet no further harm follows, the one responsible shall be fined what the woman's husband demands, paying as much as the judges determine. If any harm follows, then you shall give life for life, eye for eye, tooth for tooth, hand for hand, foot for foot, burn for burn, wound for wound, stripe for stripe. Exod. 21:22-25 NRSV**

So, "eye for eye" is clearly elliptical and means, "only the value of an eye for the loss of an eye". In other words, we have here the basis of our law of tort whereby a person can claim a right of action for damages where there has been a breach of duty. And as in the case of our law, the damages are determined by a *judge*. It is ironic that "eye for eye and tooth for tooth", which is the basis of fair compensation, is one of the most frequently misused passages of Scripture and has become a by-word for vengefulness.

Another easily misunderstood ellipsis in the O.T. is found in Exod. 20:5:

> **... For I, the LORD your God, am a jealous God visiting the iniquity of the fathers upon the children to the third and fourth generation of those who hate me.**

This appears to teach that God punishes children because of the sins of their parents. But Deut. 24:16 makes it clear that this is not the meaning:

> Fathers shall not be put to death for their children, nor shall children be put to death for their fathers, a person shall be put to death for his own sin.

These two verses are not contradictory. The clue to the meaning of Exod. 20:5 lies in the last four words, *'those that hate me'*, which are elliptical. These words relate to the *children*, as well as to their fathers. So the end of the verse means, 'visiting the iniquity of the fathers unto the third and fourth generation of their wicked children that hate me'. The implication is that the influence of bad parents tends to make bad children.

New testament divorce laws

In Matt. 19:9 we read,

> And I say to you, whoever divorces his wife, except for sexual immorality, and marries another commits adultery.

And yet in the parallel passage in Mark 10:11 we read,

> And he said to them, "Whoever divorces his wife and marries another, commits adultery against her."

Some have insisted that Mark's unqualified statement means that no follower of Christ can divorce and remarry. But Jesus did not contradict himself, so this statement in Mark must be elliptical. Mark knew that his readers would understand that sexual immorality automatically broke the marriage bond and legitimized divorce. In Luke 16:18 Jesus also omits the exceptive clause because on this occasion he was only dealing with the abuses of the Pharisees who were selling bills of divorce contrary to the spirit of the law of Moses (See ch. 25).

Those who hold extreme views on divorce also quote Rom. 7:2-3 to support their belief in the absolute indissolubility of Christian marriage:

> **1.** Or do you not know, brethren (for I speak to those who know the law), that the law has dominion over a man as long as he lives?
> **2.** For the woman who has a husband is bound by the law to her husband as long as he lives. But if the husband dies, she is released from the law of her husband.
> **3.** So then if, while her husband lives, she marries another man, she will be called an adulteress; but if her husband dies, she is free from that law, so that she is no adulteress, though she has married another man.

In this passage Paul is using death as an analogy. He reasons that just as death frees a partner from the bonds of marriage so those who have 'died' to the Law of Moses through being in Christ are freed from bondage of the Law of Moses. This is not a treatise on divorce and remarriage; it is a treatise on freedom from the Law of Moses. Paul's attribution of adultery to the woman who marries another while her husband is still alive is elliptical; it omits the fact that adultery may also break a marriage bond because this is irrelevant to the analogy.

Do we need to be baptized?

Another important example of ellipsis appears in the last message of Jesus in Mark 16:16:

> "He who believes and is baptized will be saved; but he who does not believe will be condemned."

On the basis of the second part of this verse it has been argued that baptism is not essential. However, it is clear that the negative clause in the verse is elliptical. It assumes that those who do not believe will not be baptized. That baptism is necessary is clearly stated in the parallel passage at the end of Matthew's Gospel:

> "Go therefore and make disciples of all nations, baptizing them in the name of the Father and of the

Son and of the Holy Spirit, and teaching them to obey everything that I have commanded you. And remember, I am with you always, to the end of the age." Matt. 28:19,20 NRSV

Never die?

As we have seen in chapters 1 and 16, John's writings contain many figures of speech and therefore we shall not be surprised to find that he often writes elliptically. Thus in John 11:25,26 after the death of Lazarus, Jesus comforts Martha with these words;

> **Jesus said to her, "I am the resurrection and the life. Those who believe in me, even though they die, will live and everyone who lives and believes in me will never die. Do you believe this?"** NRSV

Here Jesus was talking about the resurrection, and to understand the passage we need to insert the missing words thus — "Jesus said to her, 'I am the resurrection and the life. Those who believe in me, even though they die, will live (again, at the resurrection) and everyone who lives and believes in me will never die (eternally). Do you believe this?"

Made a curse for us

There is a passage in Gal. 3:13 which contains a highly significant elliptical statement.

> **Christ hath redeemed us from the curse of the law, being made a curse for us: for it is written, Cursed is every one that hangeth on a tree.** KJV

As it stands this statement appears to imply that anyone who was hanged on a tree, whether or not he was guilty, was cursed. However, if we look at the passage in Deut. 21 we find that although verse 23 does say that anyone hanged on a tree is accursed of God, the previous verse makes it clear that the curse applied to those who were hanged *because they had committed a capital offence* under the law.

> **22. And if a man have committed a sin worthy of death, and he be to be put to death, and thou hang him on a tree:**
> **23. His body shall not remain all night upon the tree, but thou shalt in any wise bury him that day; (for he that is hanged is accursed of God;) that thy land be not defiled, which the LORD thy God giveth thee for an inheritance. Deut. 21:22,23 KJV**

So when Paul argued that Jesus Christ had been "made a curse for us" because he had been hanged on a tree the analogy compels us to accept that in some way Jesus Christ was 'guilty' of a capital offence. How could this be since he was sinless? Peter supplies the answer in his first epistle:

> **Who his own self bare our sins in his own body on the tree, that we, being dead to sins, should live unto righteousness: by whose stripes ye were healed.**
> **1 Pet. 2:24 KJV**

Jesus Christ was *made* a curse for us because he took our sins with him to his cross. Our sins were laid on him in perfect fulfilment of the pattern of the scapegoat on whose head the sins of the people were laid before it was allowed to disappear into the wilderness (Lev. 16:21,22).

We see therefore that Paul's statement in Gal. 3:13 is elliptical. If we fill in the full implications of the statement it will read: "Christ hath redeemed us from the curse of the law, being made a curse for us (because he bare our sins in his own body on the tree): for it is written, Cursed is every one that hangeth on a tree (because such a person would have committed a sin worthy of death)."

Other examples of ellipsis occur in Rom. 5 where different interpretations have led to problems in connection with the doctrine of 'original sin', discussed in chapters 13 and 18.

We have already looked at the Hebrew comparative negative idiom (Ch.15) and it will now be evident that this idiom is elliptical. For example, when Jesus was asked to heal the daughter of a Gentile woman he said, "I was not sent except to the lost sheep of the house of Israel" (Matt. 15:24). But we know that Jesus preached to Samaritans (John 4:40) and he praised the faith of a Roman centurion (Matt. 8:10) and he declared that the temple was a 'house of prayer for all nations' (Mark 11:17). So his reply to the Syrophenician woman can be paraphrased thus: "I was not primarily sent to Gentiles; at this time my mission is to the lost sheep of the house of Israel."

Divine paradoxes

There are many other examples of elliptical statements in the Bible and by juxtaposing two elliptical statements it is possible to construct Biblical paradoxes, i.e. apparent contradictions. Here are some examples:

Bear one another's burdens (Gal. 6:2).	For every man shall bear his own burden (Gal. 6:5)
Do not love the world ... (1 John 2:15).	For God so loved the world ... (John 3:16).
If we say that we have no sin, we deceive ourselves (1 John 1:8).	Whoever has been born of God does not sin (1 John 3:9).
He who is not with me is against me (Luke 11:23).	For he who is not against us is on our side (Mark 9:40).

These apparent contradictions can be harmonized if we realize that each statement is incomplete — each expresses a truth but not the whole truth.

CHAPTER 32

PROLEPSIS

This is a figure of speech in which future events are expressed as having already happened. Since no human can predict the future with any certainty, the use of prolepsis in relation to distant historical events is a divine prerogative and is frequently found in biblical prophetic utterances. Thus in Gen. 17:5, before Isaac was born, God said to Abraham, "I have made you a father of many nations". Commenting on this statement in Rom. 4:17, Paul wrote, "God calls those things which do not exist as though they did." The Hebrew tense used in this kind of prolepsis is called a *prophetic perfect*.

Several examples of the prophetic perfect are found in Isaiah. Many years before Judah's exile Isaiah proclaimed, "My people are gone into captivity." (Isa. 5:13). In Isa. 9:6 the prophet anticipates the coming of the Messiah in these words,

> **For unto us a child is born,**
> **Unto us a son is given.**

Also, most of Isa. 53 which prophesies the suffering and death of the Messiah is expressed in the Hebrew perfect tense, as for example,

> **He was oppressed and he was afflicted,**
> **Yet he opened not his mouth;**
> **He was led as a lamb to the slaughter,**
> **And as a sheep before its shearers is silent,**
> **So he opened not his mouth.** Isa. 53:7

God of the living

A New Testament example of prolepsis is found in Luke 20:37-38 where Jesus says,

> Now even Moses showed in the burning bush passage that the dead are raised, when he called the Lord 'the God of Abraham, the God of Isaac, and the God of Jacob'. For he is not the God of the dead but of the living, for all live to him.

In this passage Jesus is contending with the Sadducees who denied resurrection. He reminded them that at the incident of the burning bush, God was proclaimed the God of Abraham, Isaac and Jacob. Since these patriarchs had been dead for hundreds of years, they would have to be raised from the dead. We know that the resurrection is still future. So when Jesus spoke of these patriarchs as 'living' he was using the prophetic perfect. He was showing the certainty of their resurrection.

These words of Jesus are sometimes quoted to show that Abraham, Isaac and Jacob were living in the spirit world when Jesus spoke, and that the resurrection is the re-entry of an immortal soul into a body. But we have already shown that the concept of an immortal soul is not found in Scripture (Chs. 13 and 16). Moreover, if the resurrection is merely the re-location of an immortal soul then it is not vitally important for our survival. Yet it is clear from 1 Cor. 15:16-18 that without resurrection we *perish*.

In N.T. times two mistaken ideas about the resurrection already existed. There were those who maintained that it had already taken place (2 Tim. 2:18), and there were others who said that it would never occur (1 Cor. 15:12). In answer to the latter Paul wrote the magnificent exposition of resurrection contained in 1 Cor. 15. There he uses sleep as a metaphor for death and describes the resurrection as occurring 'in a moment, and the twinkling of an eye, at the last trumpet!' (1 Cor. 15:52). The last trumpet is a point of time yet future which coincides with the return of the Lord Jesus Christ from heaven as described in 1 Thes. 4:16-17:

> "For the Lord himself, with a cry of command, with the archangel's call and with the sound of God's trumpet, will descend from heaven, and the dead in Christ will rise first. Then we who are alive, who are

> left, will be caught up in the clouds together with them to meet the Lord in the air; and so we will be with the Lord for ever." NRSV

This picture of the resurrection accords with the Old Testament concept expressed by Daniel:

> **Many of those who sleep in the dust of the earth shall awake, some to everlasting life, and some to shame and everlasting contempt. Dan. 12:2**

So when Jesus quoted the words of Moses at the burning bush he was speaking proleptically; he was saying, in effect, "God is not the God of mere corpses but of men and women who sleep in the grave in the sure and certain hope of being raised from the dead." It is the certainty of their resurrection which enabled Jesus to speak of Abraham, Isaac and Jacob as 'living'.

PART 3

THE STYLE AND STRUCTURE OF LANGUAGE

CHAPTER 33

PROSE AND POETRY

So far we have dealt with particular words and with figures of speech. In this third section we shall deal with the three categories of literature namely prose, poetry and drama. Prose and poetry relate to the style of the language whereas drama is structured so as to re-play speech and actions. The language of drama may be expressed in prose or poetry.

What is poetry?

It is surprisingly difficult to distinguish poetry from prose — in fact the two often merge. Prose can be poetical and poetry has been described as 'decorated prose'; in other words, language chosen for beauty as well as utility. Poetry tends to be emotional and prose factual (prosaic). In Wordsworth's familiar description, "Poetry is the spontaneous overflow of powerful feeling; it takes its origin from emotion recollected in tranquillity." For this reason poetry is usually rich in figures of speech which express feelings so much more powerfully.

Poetry also uses words for their sound effects (euphony). This 'play on words' may be alliteration which is the use of words with similar beginnings, or rhyme which is the use of words with similar endings. As a consequence poetry has been defined as 'that which is lost in translation'.

The poetry of each language can have its own characteristic structure. For example, a particular style of traditional Welsh poetry is 'cynghanedd' (metrical consonance) which uses a complicated repeated pattern of consonants within each line.

Hebrew poetry also uses repetition — in this case a repetition of ideas, usually in couplets but occasionally in triplets. The first line expresses a fact or feeling while the second or third repeats, expands or contrasts with it. This is called parallelism, as in Psa. 44:22,

> Yea, for thy sake are we killed all the day long; we are
> counted as sheep for the slaughter. KJV

But Hebrew parallelism is not simple repetition; there is some addition or intensification. It is as if the second line is saying, 'and what's more ...'. Where numbers are involved there is *augmentation* or increase as in Prov. 30:18:

> There are three things too wonderful for me,
> Yes, four which I do not understand.

In Psa. 1:1 we find *expansion*:

> Blessed is the man
> Who *walks* not in the counsel of the ungodly,
> Nor *stand*s in the path of sinners,
> Nor *sits* in the seat of the scornful.

And in Psa. 1:6 we have *contrast*:

> For the LORD knows the way of the righteous,
> But the way of the ungodly shall perish.

In addition to parallelism Hebrew poetry has a recurring rhythmical beat of accented syllables. These rhythmic assonances are, of course, only apparent if the poetry is spoken or sung in the original Hebrew language.

In the KJV the poetical sections of the O.T. are not readily distinguishable, but in the RSV and later English versions the line divisions show clearly the parallelism which provides the usual pattern for Hebrew poetry. Table 1 shows those parts of the Old Testament which are wholly or partly written as poetry. It will be seen that the first half of the O.T., up to the Book of Job, is almost entirely prose, whereas more than two thirds of the remainder is poetry:

> All of Psalms, Proverbs, Song of Solomon, Lamentations, Micah, Nahum, Obadiah, Habakkuk, Zephaniah.
>
> Most of Job, Isaiah, Hosea, Joel, Amos.
>
> Half of Jeremiah.
>
> Parts of Ecclesiastes, Ezekiel, Jonah, Zechariah.
>
> Poems within prose books include the punishments in Gen. 3; the blessings of the tribes (Gen. 49); the songs of Moses (Exod. 15), Joshua (Josh. 10), Deborah (Judg. 5) and David (2 Sam. 22); the prayer of Hannah (1 Sam. 2) and the lamentation of David (2 Sam. 1).

Table 2 Poetical Sections of the Old Testament

Perpetual Virginity?

Although it is not usually important to distinguish between poetry and prose in the O.T., there are instances where the recognition of poetry is important. For example, in Psa. 69:8,9 we have two verses which have an important bearing on the Roman Catholic doctrine of the perpetual virginity of Mary. This doctrine maintains that Mary never had sexual relations with Joseph and had no further children after the birth of Jesus. They argue that the reference to the brothers and sisters of Jesus in Matt. 13:55,56 relates to Joseph's children by former marriage.

However, in Psa. 69:8 we read concerning the Messiah,

> "I have become a stranger to my brothers,
> And an alien to my mother's children ..."

According to the rules of Hebrew parallelism the second line of the couplet complements the first so that we can be certain that the brothers of Jesus who opposed his ministry were also the children of Mary.

That this Psalm is Messianic is evident from the fact that the first line of the next verse, "It is the zeal for your house that has consumed me", is quoted in the N.T. in connection with the cleansing of the temple by Jesus. We therefore have incontrovertible evidence that the doctrine of Perpetual Virginity is unscriptural.

CHAPTER 34

POETIC HYPERBOLE

One of the commonest figures of speech in poetry is hyperbole or deliberate exaggeration, which is often expressed in metaphorical language. In most cases this is easily recognized as in a poem on the exodus where the Psalmist exclaims,

> **The sea looked and fled;**
> **Jordan turned back.**
> **The mountains skipped like rams,**
> **The hills like lambs.**
> **Psa. 114:3,4 NRSV**

Immediately after the deaths of his close friend, Jonathan, and his deadly enemy, Saul, David composed a lament that included these words, "Saul and Jonathan, beloved and lovely!" Saul was a very long way from being a lovely person! So we recognize this as poetry charged with hyperbole similar to that expressed by Jeremiah when, in the depths of despair, he cried,

> **Cursed be the day on which I was born! the day when my mother bore me, let it not be blessed! Cursed be the man who brought the news to my father, saying, "A child is born to you, a son," making him very glad. Let that man be like the cities that the LORD overthrew without pity; let him hear a cry in the morning and an alarm at noon, because he did not kill me in the womb, so my mother would have been my grave, and her womb forever great. Jer. 20:14-17 NRSV**

"The Lion shall eat Straw like the Ox"

Isa. 11 is a poetic picture of the Messianic kingdom age. The first five verses, which deal with the character and work of the Messiah are expressed in highly figurative language — mainly metaphors, such as, "stem of Jesse" "rod of his mouth".

However, when it comes to the next four verses which deal with the restoration of harmony between man and nature, the figurative language is sometimes interpreted literally, and it is suggested that in Christ's kingdom wolves will dwell with lambs, and lions will eat straw like oxen:

> **The wolf shall dwell with the lamb, and the leopard shall lie down with the kid, and the calf and the lion and the fatling together, and a little child shall lead them. The cow and the bear shall feed; their young shall lie down together; and the lion shall eat straw like the ox. Isa. 11:6-7 RSV**

Of course, it is within God's power to convert the carnivorous lion into a vegetarian animal. Such a change would involve radical alterations to the anatomy and physiology of the lion so that it would be very different from the lion of today. In order to eat straw it would need different jaws and teeth, a re-designed digestive system, important alterations to the locomotor system and re-programming of the nervous system. Moreover, it we are to suggest that all carnivores will be eliminated, then this would involve a completely new creation because it would destroy the food chains which are the basis of the delicate balance that governs the numbers and distribution of animals and plants in the world today.

Such a radical change is certainly within God's power. The question is not whether this *could* happen but whether it *will* happen. The answer will depend on whether the words are to be taken literally or as poetic hyperbole. This can be determined by comparing Scripture with Scripture because the same phrase is used in Isa. 65:25 where we read:

> "The wolf and the lamb shall feed together, The lion shall eat straw like the ox, And dust shall be the serpent's food. They shall not hurt nor destroy in all my holy mountain," Says the LORD.

The addition of the words "And dust shall be the serpent's food" indicates that the language of this vision of the kingdom of God is figurative (see Ch. 30).

The serpent eating dust is a direct reference to Gen. 3:14 and indicates that sin has been controlled. In this poetic vision of Isaiah we have a beautiful picture of Christ's Kingdom in which both peace and righteousness will prevail among men.

Joshua's Long Day

In Josh. 10:12-14 we read,

> Then Joshua spoke to the LORD in the day when the LORD delivered up the Amorites before the children of Israel, and he said in the sight of Israel:
> "Sun, stand still over Gibeon;
> And Moon, in the Valley of Aijalon."
> So the sun stood still,
> And the moon stopped,
> Till the people had revenge
> Upon their enemies.
> Is this not written in the Book of Jasher? So the sun stood still in the midst of heaven, and did not hasten to go down for about a whole day. And there has been no day like that, before it or after it, that the LORD heeded the voice of a man; for the LORD fought for Israel.

This description presents a problem because, if the sun did literally stand still, it would mean that the earth had stopped rotating. Since the linear velocity of the earth's surface at the equator is more than 1000 miles an hour and about 800 miles an hour in the latitude of Israel, the deceleration and subsequent acceleration needed to bring about a 12-hour halt would have resulted in massive tidal waves sweeping over the earth's land surfaces.

Although the moon is only one eightieth the mass of the earth, it travels round the earth at about 2300 miles an hour and it would need huge forces to stop and re-start it. But a much more important consideration is the fact that **if daylight had been extended for 12 hours then the moon would be invisible and stopping it would serve no purpose.**

Attempts have been made to explain this event in astronomical terms[1] but such speculation is unnecessary if we accept that this is another example of poetic hyperbole. In this connection we note that in the Hebrew text the halting of the sun and moon is expressed in poetry and we are informed that the words are taken from the Book of Jasher. The poetic lament of David for Saul and Jonathan in 2 Sam. 1:17-27 is also stated to be a quotation from the Book of Jasher, and in the Septuagint the two verses of poetry in 1 Kin. 8:12,13 are said to come from the "Book of Song" which probably refers to the same book of Hebrew poems or songs.

This view is reinforced by the use of a similar expression in Hab.3:10-11 which echoes the words of Joshua.

---

1. In 1950 Velikowski, a psychoanalyst with no training in astronomy or physics, published *Worlds in Collision* in which he postulated that Joshua's long day and many of the miracles connected with the exodus from Egypt and the conquest of Canaan were the result of Venus, on an elliptical orbit, repeatedly passing near to the earth.

> The mountains saw you and trembled;
> The overflowing of the water passed by.
> The deep uttered its voice,
> And lifted its hands on high.
> The sun and moon stood still in their habitation;
> At the light of your arrows they went,
> At the shining of your glittering spear.

In these verses the halting of the sun and moon are clearly set in a context of highly figurative and poetic language. The sun, moon and stars are frequently used symbolically in Scripture, and it is relevant that in the song of Deborah and Barak, following the conquest of Jabin, king of Canaan, we have another epic poem celebrating a remarkable victory which was attributed to cosmic forces.

> **They fought from heaven; the stars in their courses fought against Sisera. Judg. 5:20 KJV**

A much more likely explanation for Joshua's long day will be found if we examine the context. This epic poem was uttered by Joshua after a battle against five Amorite kings. The situation was desperate (v.6) and required an all night forced march which in those days would have required moonlight. The following day victory was helped, not by prolonging the battle, but by a miraculously timed hailstorm (v.11). It has been suggested that the reference to the sun standing still relates to the fact that after the blackness of the storm the sun burst forth and enabled the enemy to be completely routed.

Once again it must be emphasized that it is perfectly within God's power to manipulate the heavenly bodies as He sees fit. However, we find that in some of the great miracles God makes use of the laws of nature. (See footnote p.134). For example, God used a strong east wind to divide the waters of the Red Sea at the time of the exodus (Exod. 14:21) and He used an upstream landslip to block the Jordan at the time of entry into Canaan (Josh. 3:16). It would therefore be surprising if God employed a massive *cosmic* reversal just for the purpose of winning one of the many battles fought by Joshua.

Poetry in the New Testament

So far all the examples of Biblical poetry have been taken from the O.T. because nearly all the N.T. is written in prose. But there are several poetical passages in the N.T. which are either quotations from the O.T. (e.g. Luke 3:4-6, Acts 2:17-21, Heb. 8:8-12) or poetic utterances such as the annunciation (Luke 1:32-35), Mary's response (Luke 1:47-55), Zechariah's prophecy concerning John Baptist (Luke 1:67-80) and Simeon's blessing (Luke 2:29-35). The book of Revelation also contains a number of poetic passages.

What is the Holy Spirit?

Not surprisingly, the poetry of the N.T. reflects the parallelism of Hebrew O.T. poetry. In the words of Gabriel to Mary we have an interesting couplet,

> **"The Holy Spirit will come upon you, and the power of the Highest will overshadow you ..." (Luke 1:35).**

From this we learn that the Holy Spirit is a manifestation of the power of God. This parallel provides us with a useful working definition of the Holy Spirit.

CHAPTER 35

DRAMA

We have seen that there is no sharp distinction between prose and poetry. Drama, on the other hand, is a very distinct form of literature which describes events, whether real or fictional, in the form of words and actions which repeat these events as if they were actually occurring. So drama is 'action replay' and for this reason uses direct speech.

But obviously one cannot always re-play events exactly as they occurred because it would be impossible to re-create locations in every detail. Furthermore, if the events extended over a long period of time then the dramatist would have to compress the action into a much shorter time-span by eliminating irrelevant words and actions.

So the art of writing a drama involves the selection of essential details of location and action and the compression of time. This means that the dramatist, as distinct from the narrative writer, builds up the story using a sequence of 'acts' to re-create the most relevant events. Shakespeare, in his historical plays, creates vivid and penetrating pictures of the lives and characters of his subjects by re-enacting certain key events.

If confined to the action alone, a dramatist could have difficulty in conveying essential background information. For this reason a play is often introduced by a prologue to provide information about the characters in the drama and the date and location of the action. In some cases there may also be an epilogue to round off the story by giving details of subsequent events.

Since the art of the playwright is to compress as much as possible into a limited time, the words he puts into the actors' mouths must be carefully chosen for maximum impact and may not necessarily be the words of everyday speech. So the speeches in many of Shakespear's plays have a poetic quality and depth of meaning unlikely to be heard in real life.

In summary, there are four features that characterize drama, namely: 1. structure (i.e. prologue, dialogue and epilogue); 2. direct speech; 3. selection of key events; and 4. time compression. Of these features, direct speech is always present but the other devices may be present in varying degrees.

This brief analysis of the nature of dramatic writing will enable us to recognize those portions of God's word which are written in dramatic form and an appreciation of their dramatic structure will help us understand their message.

"Hast thou considered my servant Job?"

We commence with an analysis of the book of Job because it is the most obvious example of drama in the Bible. We wish to emphasize that by regarding the book of Job as a play we do not diminish its divine authority — nor do we suggest that Job was a fictional character. Drama can be a powerful means of communicating truth, and if God makes extensive use of poetry there is no reason why He should not use drama when appropriate.

Job and his friends lived in patriarchal times and the historical truth of the drama was accepted by Ezekiel (14:14) and James (5:11). The play is concerned with the problem of suffering and is based on the life story of a righteous man who was afflicted with terrible suffering.

The book has a typical dramatic structure with a prologue, three acts and an epilogue. The prologue and epilogue are written in prose whereas all the speeches in the dialogue are in poetry. This distinction is obvious when reading from the R.V. and later versions.

After introducing Job, the prologue describes how an enemy of Job's, called Satan (a Hebrew word meaning adversary, see Ch.29) argued that Job was righteous only because of the benefits it brought him. This adversary is depicted as meeting God in a court of petition and suggesting that God should test Job by bringing calamity upon him (Job

1:11, 2:5). This scenario can be understood as a dramatic presentation of the challenge facing Job in the play.

There are three acts in the drama: 1. a debate between Job and his three friends; 2. intervention by a young man, Elihu; 3. God's answer to the problem. The literary structure of the book shows we are dealing with a drama in which the speeches have been crafted by a divinely inspired dramatist. The debate is highly structured; there are three rounds of speeches, with Job alternating with each of the three friends (Table 3). No-one speaks out of sequence, there are no interruptions and all the speeches are pure poetry featuring Hebrew parallelism throughout.

Round 1	Round 2	Round 3
Job	Job	Job
|	|	|
Eliphaz	Eliphaz	Eliphaz
|	|	|
Job	Job	Job
|	|	|
Bildad	Bildad	Bildad
|	|	|
Job	Job	Job
|	|	
Zophar	Zophar	—

Table 3 Structure of the Debate

Is it conceivable that these speeches could be the actual words of a debate between a sick man and his three visitors? Can we imagine a desperately ill man replying to his critics in the most elevated poetical language? The answer to these questions must be no: unless they were all directly inspired by God. But that suggestion is negated by the fact that in the epilogue God condemns the words of Job's friends in the following words to Eliphaz:

> **My wrath is kindled against you and against your two friends for you have not spoken of me what is right, as my servant Job has.** Job 42:7 RSV

We can hardly believe that God would inspire men to speak falsehoods. It is much more likely that the speeches of the three friends are an inspired record of the false accusations that they made against him.

The drama ends with an epilogue in which God comments on the characters and we are informed that Job was subsequently blessed with the restoration of his family and property.

In the book of Job we have an important precedent. God has been pleased to reveal truths about suffering through an inspired drama. We are therefore encouraged to seek other examples of this literary genre in other parts of the inspired record.

The Song of Solomon

Solomon's Song of Songs presents some difficulties in interpretation. It could be regarded as a series of unconnected lyrics, but recurrent allusions to doves, watchmen, mountains and gardens, suggest that it should be understood as a whole.

If the book is a unity then it obviously has many of the hallmarks of drama. All except the title verse is written in direct speech; there are frequent changes of speaker — from singular to plural and from male to female; and there is interaction between the speakers or players, with questions and answers.

So the Song of Solomon appears to be a poetical drama without an explanatory prologue and without speakers' names. Several different reconstructions of the drama have been made by adding 'dramatis personae' but none can be considered authoritative.

Over and above these literary considerations there is the question of the spiritual meaning of the book which is widely regarded as an allegory of the relationship between Christ — the bridegroom, and the church — the bride. This aspect of the book will not be considered here because our purpose is only to show that the Song of Solomon is another example of inspired drama.

The Temptation of Jesus Christ

The record of the temptation of the Lord Jesus Christ in Matt. 4 and in Luke 4 is a beautiful example of dramatic writing which has all four features of this genre, namely: structure (prologue, dialogue and epilogue), direct speech, time compression and selection.

1. *Structure:* The prologue to the temptation drama informs us that the event took place immediately after Jesus was baptized, when he was led by the Spirit of God into the Judean wilderness to be tempted by the devil. This is followed by a dialogue in three acts that summarizes the events of the forty days in the wilderness. After this we have a short epilogue informing us that the temptations ceased for a period and Jesus was strengthened by the ministration of angels.

2. *Direct Speech:* The acts consist of dialogues written in direct speech. The devil in the drama could have been someone Jesus encountered in the wilderness making suggestions to Jesus as the serpent did to Eve in Eden. But this is very unlikely because there is no mountain from which the whole of the Roman world could be viewed. A more likely explanation is that the devil represents the inner voice of the human nature of Jesus against which he had to battle all his life (see Ch.30).

3. *Time Compression:* The events of the 40 days' temptation are summarized in three short acts. The statement in verses 2 of Matt. 4 and Luke 4, that Jesus was hungry after his 40-day fast, is followed by the first temptation — to make bread out of stones. This has led some to suggest that the temptations occurred at the end of the 40

days. But verses 1-2 are introductory; they are a prologue in which Luke informs us that Jesus was tempted for 40 days during which he fasted. The essential features of that 40 day ordeal are then compressed in masterly fashion into three short 'acts'.

4. *Selection:* If we analyze the nature of the three acts of temptation we find that they encapsulate the major problems with which Jesus had to battle throughout his life. As the Son of God, he had been invested with divine power through the operation of the Holy Spirit (Luke 3:22 and 4:1). The three temptations were related particularly to the possible misuse of his divine power.

In the first act he was tempted to make bread out of stones: to use his powers to satisfy personal needs. Jesus resisted with the reply that man should not live by bread alone but by every word of God. Jesus must often have been hungry but the only occasions when he used his power to create food were when he fed multitudes to whom he had first given the word of God.

In the second act he was taken to the top of a mountain from which he could see all the kingdoms of the world, i.e. the Roman Empire (Ch. 28). He was reminded that he had the power to overthrow Caesar. And with this knowledge came the temptation: why allow yourself to be crucified by the Romans when you have the power to rule the world *now*? The force of this temptation is illustrated by the incident at Caesarea Philippi when Peter vigorously denied the need for Jesus to suffer and be crucified. Recognizing the diabolical nature of this suggestion Jesus turned on Peter with the words, "Get behind me, Satan!" You are a stumbling block to me; for you are setting your mind not on divine things but on human things" (Matt. 16:23). These words are similar to his reply to the second temptation (Luke 4:8).

In the third act Jesus is taken to Jerusalem and invited to throw himself from a great height. His survival would result in instant acclamation as the Messiah. We note that not long afterwards Jesus was confronted with just such a temptation when his fellow townsfolk in Nazareth tried to throw him from a nearby precipice. He was assailed with a similar temptation when he was challenged to come down from the cross.

Each of the temptations was followed by a rejoinder from our Lord in which he quoted from the Book of Deuteronomy. Thus with infinite wisdom the inspired writer has selected three temptations to represent the most powerful forces against which Jesus had to battle and three answers which illustrate how Jesus used the sword of the Spirit, which is the word of God, to overcome these temptations.

The dramatic structure of the story of the Temptation, as related by Matthew and Luke, will be seen more clearly if we re-arrange the text as follows, using Luke's account:

The Temptations of Jesus: A Drama in Three Acts

Prologue

Jesus, full of the Holy Spirit, returned from the Jordan and was led by the Spirit into the wilderness where for forty days he was tempted by the devil. He ate nothing at all during those days, and when they were over, he was famished.

Act I — in the wilderness.

The devil: If you are the Son of God, command this stone to become bread.
Jesus: It is written, man shall not live by bread alone, but by every word of God

Act II — on a high mountain from which all the kingdoms of the world were visible.

The devil: All this authority I will give you, and the glory; for this has been delivered to me, and I give to whomever I wish. Therefore, if you will worship before me, all will be yours.

Jesus: Get behind me, Satan! For it is written, "You shall worship the Lord your God and him only you shall serve."

Act III — in Jerusalem on a pinnacle of the temple.

The devil: If you are the Son of God, throw yourself down from here. For it is written: "He shall give his angels charge over you, to keep you" and "in their hands they shall bear you up lest you dash your foot against a stone."
Jesus: It has been said, "You shall not tempt the LORD your God."

Epilogue

When the devil had finished every test, he departed from him until an opportune time.

The Song of Deborah

The Song of Deborah in Judges 5 is an epic poem celebrating the victory of the Israelites over the Midianites. In verses 28 to 30 a mini-drama records an imagined conversation between the mother of the slain Sisera and her handmaidens.

> "The mother of Sisera looked
>   through the window,
> And cried out through the lattice,
> 'Why is his chariot *so* long in coming?
> Why tarries the clatter of his chariots?'
> Her wisest ladies answered her,
> Yes, she answered herself,
> 'Are they not finding
>   and dividing the spoil:
> To every man a girl or two;

> For Sisera, plunder of dyed garments,
> Plunder of garments
>   embroidered and dyed,
> Two pieces of dyed embroidery
>   for the neck of the looter?' "
>   Judg. 5:28-30

For sheer pathos this is unequalled; it demonstrates the power of poetic drama.

These examples of dramatic writing encourage us to pursue the idea that Gen. 1 is a drama of creation. Let us look again at Gen. 1 and see how the language and structure of this chapter fit into the concept of a drama.[1]

---

1. For a more detailed consideration of this subject see *A Drama of Creation The Genesis Record and the Fossil Record*, Alan Fowler, Published by Ortho Books, High View, Litchard Rise, Bridgend, Mid Glam, CF31 1QJ, United Kingdom.

CHAPTER 36

DAYS OF CREATION

Although it is obvious that the days of Gen. 1 are 24-hour periods defined by 'evening and morning' there are widely different views on how the days should be understood.

Interpretations fall into two main groups:
A: The days are 'real time' during which God worked.
B: The days are representative or symbolic.

A: 'Real-time' days of Creation

There are three categories of interpretation in this group namely:

1. God created the heavens and the earth in six days;
2. God re-created life on earth in six days;
3. God planned his creation in six days.

1. The theory that God created the earth, sun, moon and stars in six 24-hour days less than 10,000 years ago is based on the idea that the Bible must be understood literally, but it poses severe problems for those who accept the evidence for a very old earth in the fossil record. But in spite of all the difficulties, this theory is held tenaciously by many Bible fundamentalists and will be considered in greater detail later.

2. To reconcile the fossil record with the concept that God worked for six literal days it has been suggested that the six days were the time spent by God in re-creating life on earth following a global catastrophe allegedly described in Gen. 1:2. According to this theory there is a vast time gap between verses 1 and 2. Verse 1 describes the original creation millions of years ago which gave rise to the fossil record. Verse 2 describes the effect of a catastrophe which completely wiped out this original creation, about 6000 years ago. Verses 3-28 describe how the earth was replenished over a period of six days. However, the Hebrew

text does not support this theory and there is no geological evidence for a recent simultaneous, global, catastrophic destruction of life on earth.

3. The third 'real-time' interpretation suggests that in the very beginning, over a period of six days, God devised the whole plan of creation. This 'blueprint' was later executed over millions of years of geological time.[1] Although this interpretation does not conflict with the geological evidence, it shares a problem with the other 'real-time' interpretations in that it involves God's working to a timetable based on a 24-hour 'evening and morning' time cycle. But evening and morning are only experienced by earth-bound creatures. There are no evenings and mornings with God who dwells in perpetual light (Psa. 139:12). God is outside the earth and outside our time (Psa. 90:6, 2 Pet. 3:8). God created time for man and it is inappropriate for us to suggest that His creative work was regulated by a human time-scale.

B: Representative days

The alternative to the concept of God working for six 24-hour days is to interpret the days as symbolic time-frames within which God reveals His Creation. There are two clues in the language of Gen. 1 which indicate that this is not a literal account of creation. The first is a statement in verse 22 after the creation of fish and fowl,

> **And God blessed them saying, "Be fruitful and multiply, and fill the waters in the seas, and let birds multiply on the earth."**

Here God is speaking to the fish and fowl and urging them to multiply. How can this be understood literally?

The second example of figurative language is in verse 27 where we read that "God created man in His own image". 'Image' normally relates to

---

1. A concept developed by Hugh Capron in *Conflict of Truth*, Ch.11.

the physical appearance as when Adam "begat a son in his own likeness, after his image ...". But in Gen. 1:27 'image' is clearly being used as a metaphor for character (see Ch. 3).

Guided by these language clues we shall consider briefly three symbolic interpretation of the days of Gen. 1 namely:

1. The days represent the geological periods;
2. God revealed his Creation in six days;
3. Gen. 1 is a drama of Creation.

1. The days represent geological periods.

As the Victorian geologists unearthed the history of ancient life they were impressed by some correspondence between the days of Creation and the geological periods, such as the fact that marine animals preceded land animals. From such concordances arose the idea that the days of Gen. 1 represented successive geological epochs and several books were written in the 19th century in an attempt to give scientific support to this theory.[1] However there is a major difficulty in that light appeared on the first day whereas the heavenly bodies did not appear until the 4th day. It is a profound mistake to try to construct Gen. 1 into a scientific account of geological history. The days are not chronological; they are thematic and represent various aspects of God's creative work. This becomes evident when the first three days are arranged in parallel with the second three days (Table 4).

---

1. e.g. *Work-days of God*, Herbert Morris, and *Moses and Geology*, Samuel Kinns.

Forming	Filling
Day 1. Realm of light	Day 4. Sun, moon and stars
Day 2. Sea and sky	Day 5. Fish and fowl
Day 3. Dry land and plants	Day 6. Beasts and man

Table 4   The Forming and Filling Theme of Genesis 1

The theme is 'forming' followed by 'filling'. Thus on day 1 the realm of light was formed and on day 4 it was filled with the heavenly bodies; on day 2 the realms of sea and sky were formed and on day 5 they were filled with swimming and flying creatures; on day 3 land was formed and then on day 6 it was filled with beasts, cattle, creeping things and man.

Although the days do not correspond to the geological epochs they clearly represent the many aspects of God's creative power which are encompassed by the sciences of astronomy, geology, oceanography, botany, zoology and anthropology.

2. *God revealed his creation in six days.*

This brings us to the proposition that Gen. 1 is a record of Creation being revealed in six daily visions covering various aspects of God's creation. Several suggestions have been made as to whom this revelation could have been given, including Adam, Enoch and Moses. P J Wiseman in *Creation Revealed in Six Days* (1948) produced archaeological evidence to support his theory that these visions were originally recorded on six tablets. The concept of six days of revelation is attractive because it acknowledges the fact that the days of Gen. 1 are 24 hour periods and also allows for creation to extend over vast periods of time. One difficulty with this theory is that there is no hint of visions in Gen. 1 whereas in the writings of visionary prophets such as Ezekiel and Daniel this mode of revelation is clearly stated.

A further difficulty arises from Exod. 31:17 which tells us that on the seventh day God 'rested and was refreshed'. Why should revealing creation over six days result in the need for rest and refreshment?

3. Gen. 1 is a drama of Creation.

As an alternative we would like to suggest that the representative days of creation are being presented as time frames in a drama.[1] As we have shown, the characteristics of drama are structure, direct speech, selection and time compression. The Genesis creation record has all these features. It has structure: it commences with a prologue (Gen. 1:1,2) introducing us to a dark and lifeless earth. This is followed by six acts of creation, expressed in direct speech, and it ends with an epilogue (Gen. 2:1-4) which describes the cessation of work on the seventh day and God's blessing on His creation. The work of each day is highly selective; each day represent an aspect of God's creative power. The six acts of Creation are woven into a magnificent drama which compresses the vast ages of geological time into a time frame of human dimension.

The suggestion that Genesis is a drama of creation does not imply that it is a 'play' in the ordinary sense of the word. There is no implication that Creation was acted on any kind of stage. Similarly, although the book of Job has a dramatic structure, it was obviously not intended to be performed as a stage play. Dramatic writing is essentially a literary device for the effective communication of ideas.

---

1. The closest reference to drama we have seen is in Hugo Miller, *The Testimony of the Rocks*, 1857, p.204. In his explanation of the days as representing geological epochs he suggests that Genesis 1 was "a diorama, over whose shifting pictures the curtain rose and fell six times in succession ...".

Some might question whether God would use a dramatic representation of creation to illustrate the Sabbath principle. In other words, would God use a literary device to teach a fundamental truth? The answer is yes. He does so in Heb. 7 where the example of Melchizedek is taken from Gen. 14 to demonstrate the nature of Christ's priesthood. In Gen. 14 Melchizedek appears on the scene without ancestry; there is no mention of his origin or his death. On the basis of this omission from the narrative, the writer declares that Melchizedek was "without father, without mother, without descent, having neither beginning of days nor end of life." We have no reason to suppose that this King of Jerusalem was superhuman; the N.T. writer uses this literary device to show that, unlike the Levitical priests, Christ's priesthood was not dependent on his ancestry nor was it limited by his age.

Although we believe that Gen. 1 is best understood as a drama of Creation, we accept that since God is omnipotent then all the aforementioned interpretations of Gen. 1 are possible. We cannot be dogmatic; we were not there when God created the heavens and the earth. We are not seeking what God *could* do but what God chose to do.

Must We Believe in a Young Earth?

In recent years there has been an American-led revival of Biblical literalism among Creationists who insist that there is only one valid interpretation of Gen. 1. They assert that the six 24-hour days were the time that God spent in creating the heavens and the earth and that Creation began less than 10,000 years ago. The verse which is used to underpin this literal 'real-time' interpretation of the days of Gen. 1 is Exod. 20:11 which reads:

> **For in six days the LORD made heaven and earth, the sea, and all that in them is, and rested the seventh day: wherefore the LORD blessed the sabbath day, and hallowed it. KJV**

This looks very much like a straightforward literal statement. However, when we compare Scripture with Scripture we find that this is not so, because when these words are repeated in Exod. 31:17 there is the very significant addition that afterwards God *'was refreshed'.*

> **It is a sign between me and the children of Israel for ever: for in six days the LORD made heaven and earth, and on the seventh day he rested and was refreshed   KJV.**

Yet in Isa. 40:28 we read,

> **Have you not known? Have you not heard? The everlasting God, the LORD, The Creator of the ends of the earth, neither faints nor is weary, His understanding is unsearchable.**

God, the Creator, needed neither refreshment nor sabbath rest. The sabbath was made for *man*. This is another example of *divine anthropomorphism* — the attribution of human feelings to God. Other examples are given in Ch. 26. If one part of a verse cannot be taken literally, how can we insist that the rest of the verse *must* be understood literally? It is both legitimate and reasonable to regard the 'days' in Exod. 31:17 as anthropomorphic in the same way that 'refreshed' is anthropomorphic. Since we cannot comprehend the vastness of geological time, it is appropriate that God should describe His creation within a human time frame.

Apart from the verses in Exodus which we have considered, there are no passages which suggest that the earth is very young. On the contrary there are suggestions that it is very ancient, as in Psa. 90:1-2, 102:25-27 and Job 38:4. So if Scripture is not dogmatic about the age of the earth it is surely reasonable to take into account the record of God's Creation contained in the sedimentary rocks.

The fossil record

This is not the place to give a detailed interpretation of the fossil record but a few generalizations are appropriate.

Although the fossil record consists of hard facts (fossils) there has been fierce controversy about the significance of the fossils in relation to their origins. This is mainly because the fossils have been interpreted through preconceived theories of origins which today are polarized at the two extremes of neo-Darwinism and young earth creationism. Neo-Darwinists still follow Darwin's all-or-nothing view of evolution and young earth creationists are committed to believing that nearly all the fossils were deposited following a recent world-wide flood, thus allowing no time for any significant evolutionary changes to occur.

If we approach the fossil record without prejudice we shall reach the following conclusions:

1. The earth is very old, certainly many millions of years.

2. Life on earth has appeared in the fossil record in successive bursts with rapid appearances of completely original forms of life. There have also been rapid extinctions of many forms of life.

3. Over long periods of time gradual changes have occurred, suggesting that diversification and adaptation are inherent properties of living things.

4. These minor evolutionary changes do not give rise to new organs; they only modify existing structures.

This interpretation of the fossil record accepts creation (rapid appearance) and evolution (gradual modification) but it must be emphasized that, in the fossil record, creation has the primary role; evolution only modifies created things. This concept is known a progressive creationism or old earth creationism.[1]

---

1. For a more detailed exposition of old earth creationism see Alan Hayward, *Creation and Evolution*, Triangle, 1985, and Alan Fowler, *A Drama of Creation*, op. cit.

Those who believe in a very young earth must accept the recent origin of all the fossils. So they argue that most of the sedimentary rocks and their fossils were laid down during and after a worldwide flood in the days of Noah. But anyone who walks down the Avon Gorge with a geological hammer examining the successive changes in the fossils (a sequence which is repeated worldwide in the same strata) will soon be convinced that the zoning of fossils could not have resulted from a single flood. Young earth creationists have no adequate explanation for the zoning of fossils and they cannot harmonize the fossil record with their interpretation of the Genesis record. But both these records are Divine. Gen. 1 is the word of God and the fossils are the work of God. They must agree.

Once we are freed from the dogma of young earth creationism we are able to appreciate the perfect harmony between the fossil record and the Genesis record. With the exception of Adamic man, who was created 'in the image of God', Genesis tells us nothing about the time-table of Creation nor the mechanism of Creation. Gen. 1:1 takes us back in time to an unspecified beginning and the recurrent phrase, "Let the earth bring forth", does not exclude the possibility of evolution.

By insisting that theirs is the only valid interpretation of Gen. 1, young earth creationists are inadvertently placing a stumbling-block in the path of earth scientists who will be led to believe that Gen. 1 must be mythical. Furthermore, since Jesus Christ endorsed the Genesis account of Creation (see Matt. 19:4), trust in his word may also be undermined. So literalists who sincerely believe that they are upholding the word of God are in reality turning people away from it. This is a sad irony and a very disturbing conclusion.

PART 4

VERB FORMS

CHAPTER 37

IMPRECATORY PSALMS

Of words Humpty Dumpty said, "They've a temper, some of them — particularly verbs, they're the proudest — adjectives you can do anything with, but not verbs ...".[1] In other words, verbs are the key to the meaning of a sentence. So if we are translating from a language which has verb forms with more than one mood or tense in English, this could lead to a false interpretation. Important examples of this error are found in connection with the Hebrew jussive mood and the Greek aorist tense.

The Hebrew jussive

There are some Psalms which may cause distress because of their apparently vengeful tone — even to the extent of wishing evil on the families of wicked men. For example, in Psa. 109, David says concerning his enemies,

> **5. And they have rewarded me evil for good, and hatred for my love.**
> **7. When he shall be judged, let him be condemned: and let his prayer become sin.**
> **10. Let his children be continually vagabonds, and beg: let them seek their bread also out of their desolate places. KJV**

Such words are difficult to reconcile with David's character as expressed in Psa. 51:1-3 for example, where David pours out his heart in confession of his guilt:

> **Have mercy upon me, O God, according to thy loving-kindness: according unto the multitude of thy tender mercies blot out my transgressions. Wash me**

---

1. Lewis Carroll, *Alice through the Looking Glass,* Ch.6.

> throughly from mine iniquity, and cleanse me from my
> sin. For I acknowledge my transgressions: and my sin
> is ever before me. **KJV**

Vindictiveness and cursing are no part of David's character. He was remarkably tolerant of abuse by others (2 Sam. 16:10). In the case of his most implacable enemy, Saul, David refused several opportunities to kill him and was content to await God's decision. His reliance on God is expressed in Psa. 118:7-8

> **The Lord taketh my part with them that help me:**
> **therefore shall I see my desire upon them that hate me.**
> **It is better to trust in the Lord than to put confidence**
> **in man. KJV**

The clue to the understanding of the so-called imprecatory Psalms lies in the fact that the Heb. jussive mood (used to express a strong wish — 'let something happen') has the same form as the future tense.[1] Therefore 'let his children be fatherless' could equally well be translated, 'his children will be fatherless'. So we could be reading prophecies rather than wishes and some of the imprecatory Psalms can be seen as prophetical laments for the terrible consequences of human behaviour. This is seen in Psa. 137:8-9 where the lament of the Jewish exiles in Babylon ends with a prophecy of the fate of their captors who would be conquered by the Persians:

> **O daughter of Babylon, who art to be destroyed;**
> **happy shall he be, that rewardeth thee as thou hast**
> **served us. Happy shall he be, that taketh and dasheth**
> **thy little ones against the stones. KJV**

---

1. In Hebrew the future is expressed by the imperfect tense. Davidson (*Introductory Hebrew Grammar*, T & T Clark, Edinburgh 1932, p 83) writes, 'The jussive coincides with the ordinary imperfect; and in all forms with inflectional terminations the jussive and ordinary imperfect coincide.'

These verses are a poetic lamentation on the terrible fate of Babylonian women at the hands of the Persians who would take pleasure in murdering their children.

Although the so-called imprecatory Psalms are to be seen as predicting the consequences of human wickedness, these consequences are usually brought about as a direct result of human folly. We make a great mistake if we argue that because God predicts something He is then responsible for the way it happens. The prophet Oded illustrates this in his rebuke to Israel for their slaughter of Judah:

> ... **"Look, because the LORD God of your fathers was angry with Judah, he has delivered them into your hand; but you have killed them in a rage that reaches up to heaven."** 2 Chr. 28:9

Although God had permitted Israel to punish Judah He was not responsible for their excesses.[1] God is not a puppet-master. Man has been given free-will and therefore man alone is responsible for the way in which he exercises it.

God's justice

On the other hand we cannot escape from the fact that God has the right to punish the wicked; we have to accept that in both the Old and the New Testaments there is divine justice. In Matt. 11:21-24 Jesus warns the Galilean towns who rejected him that they would be punished on the day of judgement. And in Rev. 6:10,11 white robes were given to those who "cried with a loud voice, saying, How long, O Lord, holy and true, until you judge and avenge our blood on those who dwell on the earth?"

Furthermore, it is significant that the Apostle Paul, who like David suffered from his enemies, also foresaw the day when the Lord Jesus will

---

1. The same idea is found in Zech. 1:15, RSV.

exercise divine judgement on those who oppose his rule so that they will be "punished with everlasting destruction from the presence of the Lord and from the glory of his power ..." (2 Thes. 1:9).

Such sentiments in no way contradict the principle that we should love our enemies. Jesus taught us what this means: "... bless them that curse you, do good to them that hate you, and pray for them which despitefully use you and persecute you." (Matt. 5:44). The Lord is the judge of mankind. He alone has the authority to punish. Our duty is clearly expressed by Paul in Rom. 12:19-20 (the verse in italics is quoted from Prov. 25:21-22):

> **Beloved, do not avenge yourselves, but rather give place to wrath; for it is written, "Vengeance is mine, I will repay," says the Lord.** *Therefore if your enemy is hungry, feed him; If he is thirsty, give him a drink; For in so doing you will heap coals of fire on his head.*

CHAPTER 38

THE FATAL SPEAR THRUST

The traditional view that Jesus died by crucifixion poses many problems both medical and scriptural. There are three medical problems: 1. Jesus died relatively rapidly; 2. he died with a shout; and 3. according to tradition blood flowed out of his dead body.

Scriptural problems relate to the fact that in the Old Testament the sacrifices, which were typical of Christ's sacrifice, were bled to death, whereas in the New Testament, crucifixion is a way of living — not a way of dying.

Medical Aspects

1. The piercing of hands and feet would not of itself cause significant bleeding or shock, so victims of crucifixion would normally die a very slow death from exhaustion which could take up to a week[1]. It was normal Roman practice to scourge victims before crucifixion so that Jesus was not exceptional in this respect. But he was exceptional in that he died in six hours so when Joseph of Arimathea requested the body of Jesus Pilate marvelled that he was already dead. Summoning the centurion, he asked him if Jesus had been dead for some time (Mark 15:44). Pilate would have had considerable experience of crucifixions so his surprise suggests that this was no ordinary death by crucifixion.

2. Traditionally it is accepted that Jesus died from shock and exhaustion aggravated by loss of sleep during the night of six trials. The mode of death in such circumstances would be a gradual decline in consciousness leading to coma. Anyone who has cared for a patient dying of exhaustion would know that death is gradual and is preceded by a period

---

1. However if permission were given to break the legs (*crurifrangum*) then death would quickly follow from shock due to blood loss and from asphyxia due to the weight of the body hanging on the arms and impeding chest increment.

of unconsciousness. However, the Gospels make it clear that Jesus was conscious to the very end. He died with dramatic suddenness, speaking in a loud voice just before yielding up his spirit to God.

The four Gospel records of the moment of his death are as follows:

> **Jesus, when he had cried out again with a loud voice, yielded up his spirit. (Matt. 27:50)**
>
> **And Jesus cried out with a loud voice, and breathed his last. (Mark 15:37)**
>
> **And when Jesus had cried out with a loud voice, he said, "Father, into thy hands I commend my spirit." (Luke 23:46) KJV**
>
> **So when Jesus had received the sour wine, he said, "It is finished!" And bowing his head, he gave up his spirit. (John 19:30)**

3rd hour (9 am)		1. Father forgive them ... 2. Verily I say unto thee ... 3. Woman behold thy son.	Luke 23:34 Luke 23:43 John 19:26
6th hour (12 noon)	Darkness | | |		
9th hour (3 pm)	| | Spear thrust →	4. My God, my God ... 5. I thirst. 6. It is finished. 7. Into thy hands ...	Matt. 27:46, Mark 15:34 John 19:28 John 19:30 Luke 23:46

Table 5 Seven Sayings from the Cross
At the 9th hour the last four sayings followed each other in rapid succession.

Collating the four records (Table 5) it is likely that the words "It is finished" were spoken in a loud triumphant voice followed by the words of committal in softer dying tones.

How could Jesus be so sure of the moment when he was about to die? The answer lies in a marginal note in the RV, RSV and NRSV on Matt. 27:49 which reads, **"Many ancient authorities add, And another took a spear and pierced his side and out came water and blood."**

These authorities include two of the oldest and most important codices namely the 4th century Codex Sinaiticus and Codex Vaticanus, also the important 5th century Codex Ephraemi Rescriptus.[1] The excluded words are also found in a few other Greek manuscripts, in some Palestinian Syriac manuscripts, in an old Ethiopic version and in some Latin versions and some manuscripts of the Vulgate. For reasons which we shall discuss later, very few modern translators have placed the excluded words in the text — exceptions being Ferrar Fenton and Moffatt.

If the excluded words in Matt. 27 are added to the RSV text, the narrative reads as follows:

> **And about the ninth hour Jesus cried with a loud voice, "Eli, Eli, lama sabachthani?" that is, "My God, my God, why hast thou forsaken me?" And some of the bystanders hearing it said, "This man is calling Elijah." And one of them at once ran and took a sponge, filled it with vinegar, and put it on a reed, and gave it to him to drink. But the others said, "Wait, let us see whether Elijah will come to save him." And**

---

1. Of Codex Sinaiticus and Vaticanus, Frederick Kenyon writes, "In many passages Codex Sinaiticus is found in company with Vaticanus, preserving obviously superior readings where the great mass of later manuscripts is in error." Of Codex Ephraemi he writes, "The great age of Codex Ephraemi makes it extremely valuable for the textual criticism of the New Testament." F Kenyon *Our Bible and the Ancient Manuscripts*, Eyre and Spottiswoode, 1948, pp134, 142.

> another took a spear and pierced his side, and out came water and blood. And Jesus cried again with a loud voice and yielded up his spirit. Matt. 27:46-50.

If Jesus died from this spear thrust it would explain both his early death and the fact that he remained conscious to the end.

3. Perhaps the most compelling medical evidence that Jesus died by the spear thrust is that it caused blood to flow out of his body. A corpse might produce water from an effusion of fluid into the chest cavity or from the bladder, but blood would not flow once the heart had stopped. This has always been a problem and arguments based on the fact that blood remains liquid after death are not valid because after death there is insufficient blood in the heart or major vessels to produce a flow of blood. Slaughterers of animals know that they cannot drain blood out of a dead animal. Their technique is to stun the animal and then cut the blood vessels while the heart is still beating in the unconscious beast.

Notwithstanding the weight of medical evidence, it is claimed that John 19:33,34 teaches that Jesus was pierced after death:

> **But when they came to Jesus and saw that he was already dead, they did not break his legs. But one of the soldiers pierced his side with a spear, and immediately blood and water came out.**

However the meaning of this passage hinges on the translation of the Greek aorist tense of the verb 'pierced'. In the narration of past events the Greek aorist tense may be translated into the perfect or pluperfect tense in English. So v.34 could equally well be read: **"But one of the soldiers *had pierced* his side with a spear, and immediately blood and water came out."** This verse contrasts the treatment of Jesus with that of two robbers. It is parenthetical and explains why Jesus was already dead when the soldiers came to administer the crurifragium (breaking of the legs).

The English pluperfect tense is used to translate the Greek aorist in Matt. 26:48:

> **Now his betrayer *had given* them a sign, saying, "Whomever I kiss he is the one; seize him."**

Several other examples of this use of the Greek aorist could be given such as Matt. 28:2 (KJV margin) and John 18:24 but it will suffice to look at Mark 16:1:

> **"And when the sabbath was past, Mary Magdalene, and Mary the mother of James, and Salome, *had bought* sweet spices, that they might come and anoint him." KJV**

This translation of the Greek aorist is confirmed in Luke 23:56 where we read that the women rested on the sabbath after they had prepared spices and fragrant oils.

> **And they returned, and prepared spices and ointments; and rested the sabbath day according to the commandment. Luke 23:56 KJV**

So the N.T. Greek aorist is a past tense, but not specific as to time in the past; whether it is translated as an English perfect or pluperfect depends upon the context.

Scriptural Aspects

Jesus was "the Lamb of God who takes away the sin of the world!" (John 1:29). Since he was killed at the same time as the Passover lambs were slain it is entirely appropriate that Jesus should have suffered the same mode of death as the lambs which were killed by the shedding of blood.

John tells us that the legs of Jesus were not broken on the cross in order that "the scripture should be fulfilled, Not one of his bones shall be broken" (Psa. 34:20). His bones were not broken because he was the antitype of the Passover lamb, concerning which God had said, "... nor shall you break one of its bones" (Exod. 12:46). If God had decreed an exact fulfilment of this aspect of the death of the Passover lamb, we should expect Jesus also to die by the shedding of his blood. If Jesus died by crucifixion he would not fulfil the type of the Passover lamb.

Jesus' sacrifice was also foreshadowed in the trial of Abraham, recorded in Gen. 22:1-14. Abraham said to Isaac, "God will provide a lamb." Abraham was poised to slay Isaac with a knife and doubtless intended to inflict the quickest and most humane death on Isaac by the shedding of his blood. His hand was stayed and God provided a ram whose mode of death foreshadowed that of the Lamb of God whose blood was shed by the thrust of a Roman spear.

Why were Matthew and John the only Gospel writers to mention the spear thrust and why was John so keen to emphasize that he was a trustworthy witness of the death of Jesus? John wrote,

> **And he who has seen has testified, and his testimony is true; and he knows that he is telling the truth, so that you may believe. For these things were done, that the scripture should be fulfilled, "Not one of his bones shall be broken". And again another scripture says, They shall look on him whom they pierced. John 19:35-37**

To appreciate the significance of this emphasis we should remember that, of all the disciples, John alone stood at the foot of the cross and was a first-hand witness. Moreover, we see from Table 4 that there was darkness during this time so only those standing close to the cross could see what was happening. As one of the few witnesses of the actual death of Jesus, John felt the need to emphasize that he was telling the truth and had seen the fulfilment of the prophecies concerning his bones and the piercing (Zech 12:10).

What could have been the motive for the spear thrust? There appears to be no reason for a soldier to stab the body of a dead victim of crucifixion. On the other hand no ordinary soldier would have the authority to interfere with the course of Roman justice by putting an end to the sufferings of a convicted criminal. In this connection we note that the Jews had to obtain the authority of Pilate to terminate the crucifixions by breaking the legs, but when they came to break Jesus' legs they found he was already dead (John 19:31-33).

There was, however, one person who could have been motivated to end the sufferings of Jesus and that was the Centurion in charge of the crucifixions. We read that he afterwards exclaimed, "Certainly this was a righteous man" (Luke 23:47). So it is possible that this centurion, as an act of mercy, could have ordered one of his men under cover of the darkness to put an end to Jesus' suffering. Indeed this could have been God's answer to Jesus' prayer — "My God, my God, why have you forsaken me?" Matt. 27:46 tells us that this prayer, which was the fourth of the seven sayings from the cross, was uttered at about the ninth hour (3 p.m.) shortly before Jesus died. Thus the last three sayings of Jesus from the cross followed in rapid succession (Table 5). God did not delay in responding to the despairing cry of His beloved Son.

Crucifixion: A Way of Life

The reluctance to accept the evidence that Jesus died by a spear thrust probably arises from the fact that victims of crucifixion almost invariably died by crucifixion. But Jesus was clearly exceptional. To him the cross was a symbol of self-sacrifice. He used the cross to symbolize a way of living rather than a way of dying. Crucifixion symbolized the destruction of sin-tending human nature (see Ch. 18). This explains why Jesus commands his followers to take up their crosses daily and follow him (Luke 9:23). Paul reminds the Galatians that those who are Christ's have crucified the flesh with its passions and desires (Gal. 5:24). Christ's crucifixion was therefore a public demonstration of the weakness and unprofitableness of the flesh. We are commanded to demonstrate this crucifixion in our own lives, making our bodies "a living sacrifice" (Rom. 12:1).

Redeemed by His Blood

By contrast, the death of Jesus Christ by the piercing of his side and the shedding of his blood symbolized something quite different. Jesus laid down his life for the sins of the world and paid the price of our redemption:

> **... knowing that you were not redeemed with corruptible things like silver or gold ... but with the precious blood of Christ, as of a lamb without blemish and without spot. 1 Pet. 1:18,19**

Our sins are laid on him and he alone is the slain Lamb of God who pays the ransom price for those who take up their crosses and follow him. Thus we have the solution to the age-old controversy as to whether Jesus' sacrifice was exemplary or redemptive. The answer is both. He is our example in that we are commanded to take up our crosses and follow his example of self denial (Matt. 16:24). He redeemed us in that he poured out his blood and "gave himself a ransom for all" (1 Tim. 2:6).

These two aspects of the crucifixion are symbolized in the bread and wine of the communion feast. The bread represents the body of Christ which symbolizes the body of believers (Eph. 1:22,23) who have 'crucified the flesh' by taking up their crosses daily (Luke 9:23). The wine, on the other hand, symbolizes the life-blood of our Lord poured out for us. This sacrificial death was not an example because we do not suffer his death. He alone is the sacrificial Lamb of God. His blood was shed for us and paid the full price of our redemption.

The exclusion of words in Matt. 27:49 ("And another took a spear and pierced his side and out came water and blood") may have resulted from preconceptions regarding Christ's death. It is likely that the exclusion was reinforced by the belief that the excluded words contradicted John 19:34. This again illustrates the importance of examining the language of the Bible — in this case a verb which profoundly affects our understanding of the significance of the crucifixion.

CHAPTER 39

CONCLUSION

In Part 1 we have looked at some examples to show the importance of discovering the original meanings of words in the Bible. In Part 2 we have seen how often the Bible uses figurative language and how easily misunderstandings occur. In Part 3 we have shown how the recognition of poetry and drama may also deepen our understanding and in Part 4, how the translation of verbs can profoundly affect meaning.

This prompts the question: why was the Bible written in such a way that the language often requires us to search out the meaning? In other words, why was it not always written in simple, unambiguous and literal language?

The answer lies partly in the nature of the language itself. The Bible was written by men of God who were "moved by the Holy Spirit" (2 Pet. 1:21). But although God was in full control of what was written He chose to reveal His truth through the living, vibrant language of the day. This is surely the most effective way of communicating. Would any of us try to teach our children except through the language with which they were familiar? Further, although the Bible abounds in figures of speech, this should not surprise us. No languages are 'straightforward'; all are idiomatic and use many different figures of speech because these are often the most effective way of conveying meaning. It was therefore inevitable that if God chose the best means of communicating He would speak in contemporary language.

Jesus spoke the Aramaic language of his day and frequently used metaphors and parables which are a very effective means of driving home spiritual and moral lessons. They stimulate the hearers to think for themselves by searching for the meaning and hence the injunction of Jesus, "he who has ears to hear, let him hear." Evidence for the efficacy of parables is shown by the fact that the Good Samaritan and the Prodigal Son have become metaphors for compassion and forgiveness in everyday speech.

The disciples of Jesus were sometimes baffled by his metaphors and parables — so much so that on one occasion they expressed relief when he changed to plain language (see John 16:17-32). On another occasion they asked Jesus directly, "Why do you speak to them in parables?" In reply he quoted from Isaiah 6,

> **Hearing you will hear and shall not understand,**
> **And seeing you will see and not perceive;**
> **For the hearts of this people have grown dull.**
> **Their ears are hard of hearing,**
> **And their eyes have they closed.**
> **Lest they should see with their eyes**
> **and hear with their ears,**
> **Lest they should understand with their hearts and turn,**
> **So that I should heal them.** Matt. 13:14,15

These words mean that the truth was hidden in parables because his critics had shut their eyes and closed their ears. God had not concealed the truth — their closed minds had done so. They had made up their minds and were not going to change. God was merely confirming them in the way they had determined to go.

Cynics claim that the Bible can be used to prove anything. This is only true if contexts are ignored, if no attempt is made to understand the language and if the Bible is not allowed to interpret itself.

The many conflicting interpretations of Scripture and the divisions of Christendom are no part of God's plan; they stem from the fact that God has given us free-will. We are free to decide whether or not we accept the Bible as the inspired and infallible word of God and whether we are prepared to discard our prejudices and exercise our minds in searching for its hidden treasures.

No claim to originality is made for any of our interpretations. The conclusions have been drawn from the Bible. We have merely allowed the Bible to interpret itself. We cannot do better than conclude with the words of Hubmaier the anabaptist who was martyred in 1528:[1]

> If we put beside obscure or brief passages, other passages on the same subject and bind them all together like wax candles, and light them all at once, then the clear and pure splendour of the Scriptures must shine forth.

---

1. Quoted by Alan Eyre in *The Protesters*, 1985, p.53, The Christadelphian, 404 Shaftmoor Lane, Birmingham, B28 8SZ.

INDEX OF SCRIPTURE QUOTATIONS

GENESIS
1 .... 187, 189, 192
1:1 ...... 100, 132
.... 184, 192
1:1-2 188
1:1-4 27
1:2 184
1:3-28 184
1:4 100
1:9 135
1:22 185
1:26 ...... 16, 65
1:27 ..... 29, 185-6
1:29-30 59
2:1-4 188
2:7 .... 79, 106
2:8 76
2:16-17 54
2:17 51
3 .... 146, 167
3:1 149
3:5 51
3:14 171
3:14-15 150
3:15 28
3:16 21-23
3:17-18 57
3:19 79
3:19-24 57
3:22-24 55
4:11-12 57
5:3 16
5:29 21
6:6 106

6:11 105
7:11 100
7:17-22 133
7:19-21 132
8:1 107
11:7 65
14 189
17:5 160
18:10 54
19:11 52
22:1-14 204
30:8 64
32:3 141
37:35 94
41:56 131
49 167
49:10 110

EXODUS
12:46 204
13:1-16 108
14:21 173
15 167
18:13 52
19:4 87
19:8-9 107
20:5 ...... 60, 106
.... 154, 155
20:11 189
21:22-25 154
21:28 54
23:4 54
23:12 68
26:33 64

31:17 .. 106, 188-90
32:9 87

LEVITICUS
16:21-22 158
16:34 138

NUMBERS
14:21 .... 103, 129
16:30 94
22:21-22 136

DEUTERONOMY
1:28 128
1:39 51
2:25 132
4:39 100
4:62 ...... 71, 74
6:4-9 108
6:6-9 107
7:26 54
8:19 ...... 71, 74
11:11 100
11:13-21 108
12:2 54
13:10 54
21:22-23 158-8
22:13-30 42
24:16 ..... 60, 154

JOSHUA
10 167
10:12-14 171
3:16 173

JUDGES
5 167
5:20 173
5:28-30 182
13:20 16

1 SAMUEL
1:22 13
2 167
2:30 13
14:15 64
24:3 50
25:22 50

2 SAMUEL
1 167
1:17-27 172
7:12-17 13
7:14 14
14:17 52
16:10 196
19:35 51
22 167
24:1 137

1 KINGS
2:37 54
8:12-13 172
11:14 136
12:10-11 86
22:15-16 113

2 KINGS
23:10 96

1 CHRONICLES
21:1 137
21:27 106
28:7 14

2 CHRONICLES
10:7 13
25:4 60
28:3 96
28:9 197
36:23 132

EZRA
4 138
5:1 101
6:14 101
6:15 101
6:20,21 138

NEHEMIAH
9:38 113
10:29 114
13:10 114
13:29 114
13:7-31 114

JOB
1 137
1:11 176
1:12 139
2 137
2:5 177
2:6 139
4:4-5 140
12:2 113
16:11 140
26:11 100
38:4 190
42:7 178
42:8-10 140

PSALMS
1:1 166
1:6 166

2:4 106
6:5 95
8:5 64
9:7 13
10:11 106
10:16 13
16:7 87
22:1 72
23 86
33:6-9 25
34:20 203
36:6 64
44:22 165
44:25 150
45 34
49:12 92
49:15 95
50:1 64
51:1-3 195
69:8 167
69:8-9 167
69:9 168
72:9 150
90:1-2 190
90:2 13
90:6 185
95:11 49
102 103
102:25-27 . 103, 190
109:5,7,10 195
113:6 107
114:3-4 169
115:16 77
118:7-8 196
127:2 22
137:8-9 196
139:12 185
146:3-4 .... 80, 88
146:4 107

PROVERBS
5:10 22
8 136
10:22 22
12:10 68
14:23 22
15:1 22
25:21-22 198
30:18 166
30:3 64

ECCLESIASTES
1:2 64
11:9 50

ISAIAH
1:2, 10 129
5:13 160
5:20-21 51
5:26 106
6 208
7:16 51
9:6 . . . . 34, 160
9:7 106
11:6-7 170
11:9 . . . . . 103, 129
13:10 141
14:12-13 140
14:16 141
17:10 87
32:14-15 13
38:10, 18 . . . 94-95
40:28 190
42:6-7 83
42:13 106
44:6 52
45:5-7 142
45:18 129
51:3 76
51:6 102
53:7 160
53:12 118
55:8-9 106
55:12 87
60:5 87
65:17 102
65:25 170
66:24 96

JEREMIAH
2:13 87
20:14-17 169
25:17 131
25:26 131
31:15 110
40:1 110
51:42 87
51:48 129

LAMENTATIONS
4:21 114

EZEKIEL
5:2 85
5:13 106
8:18 106
14:14 176
18:20 60
22:18 97
28:3 114
32:21 95
36:8 87

DANIEL
2:37 64
4:22 131
12:1 138
12:2 . . . 88, 99, 162

JOEL
2:30 101
2:30-31 129

AMOS
4:4-5 113

JONAH
2:2 95

HABAKKUK
2:14 . . . . . 103, 129
3:10-11 172

HAGGAI
2:14 138
2:6-7 100
2:20-23 101

ZECHARIAH
3 137-139
12:10 204

MALACHI
2:14 44
2:16 44
3 114
3:1 113
4:1 129

MATTHEW

1:1	33
1:18	34
1:18-23	26
1:25	33
2:16-18	111
3:17	36
4	179
4:2	179
5:3	82
5:5	78
5:14	27
5:32	41-43
5:34	100
5:38-45	116
5:40	117
5:44	198
7:3	128
8:6	37
8:10	159
8:11	78
8:16	82
9:6	81
9:9	144
9:13	66
9:27	143
10:8	143
10:9	123
10:10	68
10:28	70, 79, 99
11:21-24	197
11:23	101
11:23-24	95
12:24	142
12:27-28	127
12:40	73, 81, 85
12:42	131
13:3-23	147
13:14-15	208
13:41-43	75
13:44-46	75
13:55-56	167
15:19	42, 86
15:24	159
16:17	69
16:18	95
16:22	145
16:22-23	118
16:23	145, 180
16:24	206
16:27-28	81, 105
17:5	36
18:17	143
18:22	43
19:4	192
19:9	41-43, 155
21:31	144
23:24	128
23:33	151
25:34	31
26:39	35
26:45	120
26:48	203
26:52	116, 119
26:53	148
26:61	87
27	201
27:46	200, 205
27:46-50	201, 202
27:49	201, 206
27:50	200
28:2	203
28:18	30, 37
28:19-20	157

MARK

2:10-11	127
2:15	144
4:3-23	146
5:41	72
7:21-23	145, 149
8:12	82
9:40	159
9:43-48	96
10:6	18
10:11	41, 155
10:23-24	153
11:17	159
14:51-53	117
14:66-67	119
14:68	120
15:34	200
15:37	200
15:44	199
16:1	203
16:15	18
16:16	61, 156

LUKE

1:32-35	174
1:35	26, 32, 174
1:47-55	174
1:67-80	174
2:1	131
2:29-35	174
2:40	36
2:49	33
2:51-52	36
3:4-6	174
3:6	89
3:9	123
3:11	117
3:22	180
4:1	180
4:2	179
4:8	180
7:24	141

8:4-15 147	**JOHN**	10:30-36 3
8:26 127	1:1-4 25-27	10:34-36 12
8:55 82	1:1-5 24	10:36 32
9:3 117	1:9-10 27	11:11-14 3
9:23 205-206	1:10 27	11:12 87
9:60 87	1:14 . . . . 26, 89	11:25-26 157
10:6 74	1:29 203	11:53 125
10:20 70	2:16 38	12:6 . . . . . 123, 145
11:23 159	2:19 . . . . 3, 87	12:10 125
13:28 78	2:21 3	13:2 145
14:12 66	3:4 87	14:2 38
14:26 67	3:5-10 3	14:2-3 85
15:24 87	3:8 82	14:3 39
16:1-10 121	3:13 . . . . . . 78, 100	14:6 61
16:9 122-123	3:14-15 151	14:16 14
16:14 123	3:16 159	14:16-17 39
16:16 . . . . 75, 123	4:10-11 27	14:23 39
16:18 . . . . . 41, 123	4:10-14 3	14:23-26 40
18:30 14	4:15 87	14:26 6
19:22 126	4:20 138	15:1 87
19:22-23 126	4:22 27	15:26 40
20:37-38 160	4:40 159	16:7 40
20:47 123	4:42 70	16:13 40
21:24-27 101	5:18 32	16:16 40
21:25 87	5:19 32	16:16-29 4
22:18 75	6:27 66	16:17-32 208
22:31 118	6:35 87	16:21 23
22:36-37 118	6:51-57 3	16:25-29 108
22:36-38 116	6:53 88	17:14 31
22:39-46 148	6:54 14	17:20-22 33
23:34 200	6:66 75	18:24 203
23:43 . . 71, 73, 200	6:70 144	18:25 120
23:46 200	8:15 28	18:31 115
23:47 205	8:21-30 3	18:37 49
23:56 203	8:23 27	19:6 115
24:6 81	8:28 34	19:26 200
24:21 39	8:44 146	19:28 200
24:37 82	8:56 28	19:30 200
24:39 89	10:30 32	19:31-33 205

19:33-34 202	6:23 . . . . 56, 62	15:25-28 30
19:34 206	7:2-3 155	15:27 36
19:35-37 204	7:3 41	15:39 89
21:7 117	8:1 89	15:50 69
21:22-23 4	8:3 90	15:51-54 79
21:25 . . . . 27, 128	8:5-6 90	15:52 161
	8:7 90	15:53 55
ACTS	8:11-13 82	15:56 . . . . . 63, 151
1:6 . . . . 39, 75	8:13 91	
2:4-6 111	8:18-23 19	**2 CORINTHIANS**
2:5 132	8:22 18	3:18 29
2:11 112	8:22-23 20	4:6 27
2:16 129	8:29 30	5:17 19
2:17-21 174	8:39 18	6:16 38
2:19 102	11:33 106	7:1 90
2:19-20 129	12:1 205	11:14 146
2:27 . . . . 81, 95	12:19-20 198	11:16-21 114
2:34 77	15:5 107	12:1-4 77
4:29-30 37		12:13 114
5:3 . . . . . . 143, 146	**1 CORINTHIANS**	
8:30 3	1:17 66	**GALATIANS**
10:29 24	2:13 6	1:16 69
11:28 131	2:14 145	2:7-9 110
	5:1 42	3:13 157,158
ROMANS	6:4 114	3:24 28
1:4 29	6:18 42	4:22-31 109
1:20 . . . . 18, 27	7:10-11 44	5:2 153
1:23 17	9:9-10 67	5:19-21 92
1:25 18	9:27 15	5:24 205
2:4 107	10:2 138	6:2 159
2:7 . . . . 63, 80	14 . . . . . . 111, 112	6:5 159
3:9-10 63	14:22 111	6:15 19
4:17 . . . . . . 31, 160	14:23 112	
5:12 58	15 161	**EPHESIANS**
5:12-21 61	15:12 161	1:3 69
5:13-14 62	15:16-18 161	1:4 31
5:15-21 61	15:20 29	1:20 69
6:4 152	15:24-28 105	1:20-22 30

1:22-23 206	**2 TIMOTHY**	**JAMES**
2:2 143	2:18 161	5:11 176
3:9-11 30	3:3 144	
3:10 69	4:1 75	**1 PETER**
5:30 87	4:8 78	1:4 78
6:11 146		1:10-11 83
6:12 ..... 69, 143	**TITUS**	1:18-19 206
6:20 69	1:2 15	2:13 18
	2:3 144	2:24 158
PHILIPPIANS		3:15 24
2:5-6 53	**HEBREWS**	3:18-20 82
	1:1-2 28	3:19 84
COLOSSIANS	1:2 28	3:21 .... 70, 83, 90
1:15 .... 16, 19, 30	1:4 28	4:7 104
1:15-16 28	1:5 14	4:13 78
1:16 30	1:8-9 34	5:13 118
1:18 29	1:10-11 102	5:8 146
1:23 ...... 18, 132	1:10-12 103	
2:18 90	1:14 82	**2 PETER**
3:10 17	2:14 ... 69, 91, 143	1:21 .... 6, 207
3:12 86	.... 148, 151-2	2:5 .... 84, 105, 135
	2:14-17 .. 33, 80, 91	3:5-6 134
1 THESSALONIANS	2:14-18 35	3:5-13 77
4:3 42	2:18 91	3:7-14 103-5
4:16-17 161	3:6 38	3:8 ..... 107, 185
	3:13 146	3:10 128
2 THESSALONIANS	4:3 49	
1:9 198	4:13 19	**1 JOHN**
2:8 82	5:7-9 35	1:8 159
	6:5 102	2:15 159
1 TIMOTHY	7 189	3:9 159
1:17 55	7:26 151-2	4:1 83
2:6 206	8:8-12 173	5:13 14
2:9-10 70	9:11 18	
2:14 57	10:1 ...... 27, 103	**JUDE**
3:7 146	11:9 123	9 138
5:17-18 68	12:2 151	14-15 84
6:16 ...... 55, 77	12:23 29	23 139
.... 79, 100	12:25-28 .. 101, 102	

217

REVELATION
1:8 31
1:18 95
2:2, 12 63
2:7 . . . . 55, 76
6:10-11 197
11:18 . . . . . 76, 130
12:9 . . . . . 139, 144
13:8 31
13:18 55
20:2 . . . . . 143, 149
20:6 14
20:14 99
21:4 99
22:2 . . . . 62, 63
22:1-5 56
22:12 78

218